boards, platters, plates

RECIPES FOR ENTERTAINING, SHARING, AND SNACKING

Maria Zizka

Photographs by Erin Scott

ARTISAN | NEW YORK

Library of Congress Cataloging-in-Publication Data

Names: Zizka, Maria, author. | Scott, Erin, photographer.
Title: Boards, Platters, Plates : Recipes for Entertaining, Sharing, and Snacking / Maria Zizka ; photographs by Erin Scott.
Description: New York, NY : Artisan, a division of Workman Publishing Co., Inc., [2021] | Includes index.
Identifiers: LCCN 2020042990 | ISBN 9781579659929 (hardcover)
Subjects: LCSH: Cooking. | Snack foods. | Entertaining. | LCGFT: Cookbooks.
Classification: LCC TX714 .Z59 2021 | DDC 641.5—dc23
LC record available at https://lccn.loc.gov/2020042990

Design by Suet Chong

Artisan books are available at special discounts when purchased in bulk for premiums and sales promotions as well as for fund-raising or educational use. Special editions or book excerpts also can be created to specification. For details, contact the Special Sales Director at the address below, or send an e-mail to specialmarkets@workman.com.

For speaking engagements, contact speakersbureau@workman.com.

Published by Artisan
A division of Workman Publishing Co., Inc.
225 Varick Street
New York, NY 10014-4381
artisanbooks.com

Artisan is a registered trademark of Workman Publishing Co., Inc.

Published simultaneously in Canada by Thomas Allen & Son, Limited

Printed in China

10 9 8 7 6 5 4 3

for graham

CONTENTS

to start

vegetable-focused

49
Mostly-Vegetables Chicken Salad Crostini
radish-cucumber-chicken salad + leafy green tangle + country-style bread + grapes

51
Lebanese Lunch
hummus + muhammara + labne + radishes + olive-oil marinated cheese + pita bread

56
From the Garden
* *party size* *
beet dip with pine nut crunch + lemon-basil white bean dip + quick pickles + honeyed ricotta + prosciutto and melon + seeded crackers

61
When in Rome
fresh mozzarella and cherry tomato bites + pistachio pesto + olive tapenade + focaccia

63
Green Goddess
"grilled" vegetables + green goddess sauce + seven-minute eggs + flatbread crackers

68
Vegan Rainbow
vegan rainbow rolls + peanut dipping sauce + jicama + pineapple + vegetable chips

all-day

73
DIY Hoagie Bar
cured meats + provolone + spicy pepper mayonnaise + iceberg slaw + sesame loaf

75
Tiny Baked Potato Poppers
baked new potatoes + real bacon bits + garlic-chive butter + sour cream

79
Chips and Crispy Chickpeas
pita chips + crispy chickpeas + harissa-sumac sauce + manouri cheese + black olives

81
Onigiri
steamed rice + spicy tuna filling + nori + shichimi togarashi + edamame

86
Summertime Bagna Cauda
* *party size* *
Parmigiano twists + garlic-anchovy dipping sauce + balsamic vinegar dip + summer vegetables + Italian cheeses

91
Le Grand Aioli
aioli + haricots verts + boiled potatoes + Niçoise olives + shrimp + seven-minute eggs

cocktail parties

98
New Year's Eve
✳ party size ✳
bite-size latkes + homemade applesauce + sour cream + smoked salmon + sliced cucumber + dill

103
The 007
oysters on the half shell + vodka mignonette sauce + lemony frisée + buttered toast

107
Korean BBQ
bulgogi-style beef + lettuce cups with so many herbs + gochujang dipping sauce + kimchi

112
Chicken Dinner
✳ party size ✳
popcorn chicken + cornbread bites + hot honey + homemade ranch + carrots and celery + cabbage ribbons

117
Smørrebrød-esque
smoked salmon + caper berry cream cheese spread + pickled green onions + crackers

119
Spicy Herby Kofta
lamb kofta + yogurt-mint sauce + herb salad + pita bread

sweet

125
Holiday Cookie Swap
lemon-rosemary shortbread + chocolate bark + gluten-free coconut macaroons

130
Chocolate Deluxe
✳ party size ✳
tahini swirl brownies + chocolate-dipped strawberries + chocolate-hazelnut spread + pretzels + dark chocolate truffles + chocolate–peanut butter cups + mixed nuts + figs + plums

135
Autumn Harvest
sugared grapes + green apples + salted caramel sauce + candied walnut crunch

139
S'mores Without a Campfire
graham crackers + toasted marshmallows + warm chocolate sauce

141
High Tea
hibiscus-glazed scones + barely whipped cream + berry jam + fresh fruit

145
Honey and Halva
halva-stuffed dates + honeycomb + baklava + figs

INTRODUCTION

Enjoying a meal on a board starts off with appreciation for the food's beauty: ripe fruit cut into bite-size pieces begging to be picked up, crunchy seeded crackers peeking out from behind paper-thin slices of prosciutto folded like billowy linens, creamy dips with warm breads to drag through them. The presentation of the board gives you flexibility in how you go about enjoying it. You can jump around from component to component, a bite of this followed by a bite of that, or home in on one element at a time. There are no rules to creating a board—you can have dips and spreads, sandwiches and sliders, vegetables or fruits—but in a well-crafted board, everything goes together. And boards are fun; you eat with your hands, not a fork and knife.

Putting together a board is cooking, for sure, but it often feels more like a combination of foraging, matchmaking, and composing. The hardest part is usually gathering all the delicious ingredients. Here are some guidelines to keep in mind:

1. **LOOKS MATTER.** We eat with our eyes first, so make sure to consider a board's appearance. Arrange the multiple

components in a natural way (i.e., composed but not painstakingly tweezered into place). Keep it real and let the food fall where it falls, especially if that happens to be a little off the edge. Whenever possible, choose a medley of colorful ingredients.

2. **STAY FLEXIBLE.** Part of the beauty of a good board is that it can sit out on your table for a couple of hours without wilting or getting cold. Most board foods aren't too temperature sensitive, and if they are, you can always keep them well chilled by serving them on a bed of crushed ice, like oysters on the half shell.

3. **MAKE IT FUN TO EAT.** Boards are interactive and shouldn't require plates or utensils. All you need are your hands or maybe a toothpick. And go for dips galore, because who doesn't love dipping?

4. **EMBRACE STORE-BOUGHT COMPONENTS.** A board should have a variety of components—ideally three or more—but nobody has all day to cook everything from scratch. Assembling a board ought to be less time-consuming than cooking a multicourse meal. That's where store-bought ingredients come in. Most avid cooks will tell you that homemade foods are superior to their supermarket counterparts. But there are countless exceptions to this rule: crunchy candied walnuts, spicy harissa, specialty crackers of all types (seeded, flatbread-style, whole-wheat), jarred roasted peppers, and berry jam, just to name a few. Many of these store-bought foods are right

at home on a board. They might not be the centerpiece component, but they do help make a board more bountiful, without asking for hardly any of your time.

On the topic of store-bought ingredients, whether you're buying fruits and vegetables or a bag of tortilla chips, always choose the highest-quality ingredients you can afford. Buy fresh breads, cookies, and pastries (like baklava for the Honey and Halva board, page 145) from local bakeries whenever possible. Read the labels on packaged items carefully. Avoid stabilizers, artificial colors, and chemicals with unpronounceable names. For tinned fish like anchovies and tuna, opt for sustainably caught fish packed in 100 percent extra-virgin olive oil. Buy cheeses and smoked fish from local shops, if you can, or consider ordering online. Check Sources (page 149) for some favorite store-bought brands to try, and embrace the search for producers that you admire and trust.

Determining a board's precise yield is tricky. Much depends on the eater(s) and the occasion. Sometimes, you might want to make a board as a complete meal. Other times, you might assemble two or three boards and serve them together to friends. Most of the recipes in this book serve two hungry people. All the recipes scale easily; you can double or triple the quantities for a single component, or you can fill out a board by including additional components such as a sliced avocado or a few bunches of grapes. If you're gathering with a group, check out the party-size boards for feasts to feed eight to ten people.

Please don't be afraid to substitute ingredients. Make the most of gorgeous seasonal produce. If sweet peppers look especially perky at the market, go ahead and use them in place of the radishes in the Mostly-Vegetables Chicken Salad Crostini (page 49). During winter, try swapping sliced fennel for the sugar snap peas in Summertime Bagna Cauda (page 86). And always follow your taste buds. If you love spicy foods, add a pinch (or three!) of cayenne to the batter for Chicken Dinner (page 112).

On the following pages, you'll discover recipes for all kinds of boards, from snacky options like Aperitivo (page 25) to savory spreads that are perfect for a cocktail party like The 007 (page 103) and Spicy Herby Kofta (page 119). There's even a whole chapter dedicated to dessert boards filled with sweets. There are also make-ahead and storage tips, plus suggestions for how to repurpose any leftovers. Let these recipes serve as jumping-off points, inspiring you to make delicious, beautiful, bountiful boards from your favorite ingredients.

the cheese board

Cheese and charcuterie boards are the granddaddies of all boards. Learning how to assemble one is a good lesson in assembling any board. You'll notice some of the themes outlined here apply to all boards. For example, a variety of colors and textures is always ideal. Also, remember to think about how each component will be eaten, then include any necessary accoutrements (like small knives or spoons or an empty bowl for olive pits).

- Anchor the board with a triangle of three different cheeses: one cow-milk cheese, one sheep-milk cheese, and one goat-milk cheese.
- Aim for a variety of colors (cream, blue, straw yellow) and textures (soft, semisoft, firm).
- Estimate about 2 ounces of cheese total per person.
- Supply a separate serving utensil for each cheese—it doesn't have to be a fancy cheese service set; a small knife is ideal for most textures.
- Let the cheese warm up at room temperature for at least one hour before serving, because cold temperatures dull flavors.
- Place accompanying components in the empty spaces on the board.

Manchego

marinated olives

crackers

fresh fruit

cornichons

honey

Gouda

Marcona almonds

goat cheese

dried
fruit

the charcuterie board

- Choose three different meats:
  - › one whole salami in the classic baton shape with its white protective mold coating; it could be Italian soppressata, finocchiona, or Genoa or Spanish chorizo or French saucisson sec. You'll need to supply a sharp knife to slice it. Start by cutting only eight or so slices, leaving the rest of the salami whole (for the best-looking presentation).
  - › one very thinly sliced cured meat, like prosciutto, coppa, or even lardo
  - › and one charcuterie with a soft, spreadable texture, such as 'nduja
- Balance the richness of the charcuterie with a crunchy, tangy, pickled component like whole caper berries.
- Offer crackers or bread, which are essential.
- For a great accent, place a small container of whole-grain mustard on the board.
- And just for fun, consider including a surprise element—something you and your friends might not be super familiar with, such as green almonds.

'nduja

soppressata

whole-grain
mustard

crackers

prosciutto

green
almonds

caper
berries

to start

aperitivo

frizzled shallot dip + potato chips + Marcona almonds + olives

Serves 2 to 4 • Inspired by the Italian ritual of a predinner snack, this board has a couple of components you might expect (olives and salty almonds), but it also has a riff on sour cream–and–onion dip that's made with frizzled shallots and the thick strained yogurt called labne. Sour cream is an easy substitute if you can't find labne, but the labne is better because it's thicker and creamier.

FRIZZLED SHALLOT DIP

Makes about 1 cup (225 g)

1 large or 2 small shallots, peeled and very thinly sliced

½ cup (120 ml) vegetable oil

Fine sea salt

1 cup (225 g) labne or sour cream

2 tablespoons fresh lemon juice

Freshly ground black pepper

1 tablespoon finely chopped chives

STORE-BOUGHT COMPONENTS

Dill pickle potato chips or sea salt potato chips

Marcona almonds, Guara almonds, or salted roasted almonds

Castelvetrano olives or other olives with pits

Make the frizzled shallot dip: Line a plate with paper towels or a clean brown paper bag. Place the shallots in a small saucepan and pour in the vegetable oil. Cook over medium-low heat, stirring occasionally, until the shallots are mostly brown, 10 to 12 minutes. Strain the fried shallots through a fine-mesh sieve, and then spread them out on the prepared plate. Sprinkle them with a pinch of salt. (Save the flavorful shallot oil for another recipe, like Korean BBQ on page 107.)

In a medium bowl, stir together the labne, lemon juice, and frizzled shallots. Taste and season with salt and pepper.

Spoon the frizzled shallot dip into a small bowl and top with the chopped chives. Place the bowl on the serving board, with the potato chips alongside. Set the Marcona almonds on the board as well. Place the mixed olives on the board (and don't forget to set out a tiny bowl for pits!).

catalonian summer

romesco + charred green onions + anchovy toasts + Manchego

Serves 2 to 4 • Romesco is a bright orangey-red Catalonian sauce made from roasted peppers, tomatoes, and ground almonds. It's a delicious dip for charred green onions, and you can make what I consider a perfect bite by combining the two on an anchovy toast with a thin slice of Manchego cheese.

ROMESCO

Makes about 1½ cups (350 g)

1 (8-ounce/225 g) jar of roasted peppers, drained and rinsed

4 oil-packed sun-dried tomatoes, drained and rinsed

¼ cup (35 g) salted roasted almonds or Marcona almonds

1 garlic clove

2 teaspoons sherry vinegar or red wine vinegar

½ teaspoon smoked paprika (sweet or hot)

Pinch of chile flakes

Fine sea salt

¼ cup (60 ml) extra-virgin olive oil

CHARRED GREEN ONIONS

1 tablespoon extra-virgin olive oil

6 green onions, cut into 3-inch (7.5 cm) segments

Flaky sea salt

ANCHOVY TOASTS

6 anchovy fillets, rinsed

1 tablespoon sherry vinegar or red wine vinegar

2 thick slices of country-style bread (like rustic sourdough)

Extra-virgin olive oil

Freshly ground black pepper

STORE-BOUGHT COMPONENTS

Manchego cheese (or any firm sheep-milk cheese), thinly sliced

Make the romesco: In a food processor, blend the roasted peppers, tomatoes, almonds, garlic, vinegar, paprika, chile flakes, and ½ teaspoon of fine salt until combined. While the machine is spinning, slowly pour in the olive oil and blend until smooth, 10 to 30 seconds. Taste and season with more salt if needed and a little more chile flakes if you'd like the sauce to be spicier. Spoon the romesco into a small serving bowl.

Char the green onions: Heat a large cast-iron skillet over high heat for 3 minutes. Swirl in the olive oil and place the green onions in the pan. Cook, turning the onions once or twice, until completely tender and charred in some places, about 4 minutes. Transfer to a small plate and season with 2 pinches of flaky salt.

Make the anchovy toasts: Place the anchovies in a small dish and pour in the vinegar. Let marinate for about 5 minutes and up to 1 hour. Toast the bread well until the edges are browned but not burned. Drizzle the bread with olive oil and then cut each slice on an angle into 3 or 4 equal-size pieces. Drape 1 marinated anchovy over each piece of toast. Season generously with pepper.

Assemble: Arrange the anchovy toasts on one side of the board. Place the bowl of romesco in the middle of the board, with the plate of charred green onions next to it. Set the sliced Manchego on the other side.

parisienne, see page 32

parisienne

tiny roasted summer squash–and–goat cheese sandwiches + tiny ham-and-butter sandwiches + seven-minute eggs + radishes

+ Comté + cornichons

Serves 8 to 10 · Tiny two-bite sandwiches are pretty cute and fun to eat. You can't go wrong following the French lead with a baguette, a generous amount of salted butter, and good-quality ham. If you only have unsalted butter on hand, sprinkle a little flaky salt over the butter when you're assembling the sandwiches. The other tiny sandwich with roasted squash and goat cheese is a nice option for vegetarians.

SEVEN-MINUTE EGGS

6 large eggs

ROASTED SUMMER SQUASH–AND–GOAT CHEESE SANDWICHES

3 or 4 small long summer squash (about 1 pound/455 g), sliced crosswise into ¼-inch (6 mm) rounds

3 tablespoons extra-virgin olive oil

Fine sea salt

Freshly ground black pepper

1 baguette

4 ounces (115 g) fresh goat cheese (the kind with herbs is nice!)

2 tablespoons fresh oregano leaves

2 tablespoons chopped fresh dill

HAM-AND-BUTTER SANDWICHES

1 baguette

4 to 6 tablespoons (55 to 85 g) really good salted butter, at room temperature

8 ounces (225 g) jambon de Paris or other good-quality ham, sliced paper-thin

STORE-BOUGHT
COMPONENTS

2 bunches of radishes,
trimmed and cut into
halves or quarters

1 large wedge of
Comté or other firm
French cheese

1 small jar
of cornichons

Cook the eggs: Bring a medium saucepan of water to a boil. Carefully lower in the eggs, adjust the heat so that the water simmers gently, and cook for exactly 7 minutes. (If you're starting with fridge-cold eggs, after 7 minutes of cooking time, the whites will be set but the yolks will still be soft and a little runny in the centers; if you prefer yolks that are fully set, cook the eggs for 10 minutes total.) Transfer the cooked eggs to a bowl of ice water and let cool for 2 minutes, then crack and peel away the shells.

Make the squash sandwiches: Heat the oven to 400°F (200°C). Place the squash rounds in a single layer on a baking sheet, drizzle with the oil, and sprinkle with salt and pepper. Roast, turning once, until the squash is tender and golden brown in a few places, about 25 minutes.

Using a sharp serrated knife, carefully slice the baguette lengthwise. Place the two halves cut-side up. Spread the goat cheese evenly across both halves, then tile the roasted squash rounds on top of the cheese. Scatter the herbs and slice the sandwich crosswise into two-bite portions.

Make the ham sandwiches: Using a sharp serrated knife, carefully slice the baguette lengthwise. Place the two halves cut-side up. Spread the butter evenly across both halves. Drape the ham over the butter, and then slice the sandwich crosswise into two-bite portions.

Assemble: Place the tiny sandwiches on one side of a large board. Cut the peeled eggs into halves, season with salt and pepper, and arrange them next to the sandwiches. Set the radishes, Comté, and cornichons alongside (with a small fork for spearing the cornichons and a small knife for serving the cheese).

The radishes and cornichons are nice to pick up and crunch on to cleanse your palate between bites of the more structured tiny sandwiches. And the cheese is just great to have on this board because it's cheese!

new fondue

baked cheese + garlic-rubbed baguette croutons + chicories + fig jam + apricots

Serves 2 to 4 • You can make this new take on fondue with any whole wheel of soft-ripened cheese like Brie, Camembert, or Cambozola. Little 4-ounce (115 g) wheels are ideal for two servings, but don't worry if your cheese is larger or smaller—the cooking method is the same. For a fun alternative to this recipe, use apricot jam and fresh figs, or come up with your own combo of fresh fruit and cooked fruit.

BAKED CHEESE

1 (4-ounce/115 g) whole soft-ripened cheese (such as Brie, Camembert, or Cambozola)

1 garlic clove, thinly sliced

2 sprigs of thyme

1 teaspoon honey

GARLIC CROUTONS

¼ baguette

1 tablespoon extra-virgin olive oil

Flaky sea salt

1 garlic clove

CHICORIES

½ small head of radicchio (about 2 ounces/55 g) or other bitter salad green like escarole

1 teaspoon fresh lemon juice

1 teaspoon red wine vinegar

Flaky sea salt

Freshly ground black pepper

Extra-virgin olive oil

STORE-BOUGHT COMPONENTS

Fig jam or other preserves

Apricots, halved or quartered if large, or other fresh fruit

Make the baked cheese and croutons: Heat the oven to 400°F (200°C).

If the cheese came in a wooden box, remove it and discard any plastic or wax paper wrapping. Place the cheese in a ramekin or small baking dish. Use the tip of a knife to score a crosshatch pattern in the top. Insert the slices of garlic into the cheese and lay the thyme sprigs on top. Drizzle the honey over the cheese. Set the ramekin on a baking sheet and set aside.

Cut the baguette into ¼-inch (6 mm) slices. Spread them out in a single layer on the baking sheet alongside the cheese. Drizzle the bread evenly with the oil and sprinkle with a few pinches of flaky salt.

Place the baking sheet in the oven and bake until the croutons are golden brown and the cheese is gooey, 10 to 12 minutes. Flip the bread after 5 minutes for even browning. When the croutons are done, rub them with the garlic clove while they are still hot. The cheese might need a few more minutes to get nicely browned and bubbly around the edges.

Dress the chicories: Just before you're ready to serve, pull apart the radicchio into individual leaves and cut or tear any large leaves into pieces about the size of a tortilla chip. Toss the leaves with the lemon juice and vinegar in a large bowl. Season with flaky salt and pepper to taste. Drizzle with oil and toss gently to coat.

Assemble: Set the baked cheese (still in its ramekin) on a board. Spoon some fig jam on top of the cheese. Arrange the croutons, chicories, and apricots on the board. Everything can be dipped into the melty cheese except the apricots, which are a lovely sweet counterpoint between salty bites.

cauliflower pakoras and friends

| cauliflower pakoras | + | yogurt-mint sauce | + | mango chutney | + | masala cashews |

Serves 2 to 4 • These gluten-free cauliflower fritters are fantastic dipped into a duo of complementary sauces. The yogurt-mint sauce doesn't take too long to make, but if you don't have the time or desire, simply stir some finely chopped mint leaves and a big squeeze of lime juice into thick Greek yogurt; season with salt and pepper for the simplest (and maybe best) dipping sauce.

CAULIFLOWER PAKORAS

1 quart (960 ml) vegetable oil, for frying

¼ cup (25 g) chickpea flour

¼ cup (30 g) white or brown rice flour

¼ teaspoon baking soda

½ teaspoon garam masala

¼ teaspoon fine sea salt

5 to 7 tablespoons (75 to 105 ml) sparkling water

¾ small head of cauliflower (about 1 pound/455 g), cut into bite-size florets

Flaky sea salt

½ cup (125 g) Yogurt-Mint Sauce (page 119)

STORE-BOUGHT COMPONENTS

Masala cashews or other roasted nuts

1 lemon, cut into wedges

Mango chutney

Make the cauliflower pakoras: In a heavy-bottomed pot, pour the vegetable oil (enough to fill your pot with at least 3 inches/7.5 cm of oil) and heat to 350°F (180°C). Use a probe-style instant-read thermometer to test the heat of your oil. If you don't have a thermometer, stick the handle of a wooden spoon into the oil; if bubbles form around the wood and float to the surface, the oil is ready. The oil usually takes somewhere around 10 minutes to heat.

While the oil heats up, whisk together the chickpea flour, rice flour, baking soda, garam masala, and fine salt in a large bowl. Gradually pour in the sparkling water, 1 tablespoon at a time, adding only as much water as needed for the batter to have the consistency of unwhipped heavy whipping cream. Add the cauliflower to the batter and mix well.

Line a plate with paper towels or a clean brown paper bag and set aside. When the oil is ready, carefully lower about half of the cauliflower florets into the hot oil so that they are not crowded in the pot. Fry without stirring for 2 minutes or so, until the batter sets. Then give the florets a stir and continue to fry until golden brown, about 5 minutes total. Use a slotted spoon to transfer the pakoras to the prepared plate. Season generously with flaky salt. Repeat this process to fry the remaining cauliflower, checking the temperature of the oil in between batches and adjusting the heat as needed to keep the oil at a steady 350°F (180°C).

Assemble: Arrange the cauliflower pakoras on a board with the masala cashews. Set the lemon wedges alongside for squeezing on the pakoras. Serve the yogurt-mint sauce and mango chutney in separate small bowls next to the pakoras for dipping.

beachside vacation, see page 44

beachside vacation

chilled pickled shrimp + tortilla chips + mango-jalapeño salsa + avocado

Serves 2 to 4 ▪ Chilled pickled shrimp are especially refreshing, and when served alongside tortilla chips and mango-jalapeño salsa, they turn what would be just a snack into a whole meal. Add as much jalapeño as you like to the mango salsa to adjust the heat level.

PICKLED SHRIMP

Handful of ice cubes

2 garlic cloves, thinly sliced

1 small dried hot chile, or ¼ teaspoon chile flakes

3 tablespoons apple cider vinegar or white wine vinegar

1 tablespoon fresh lemon juice

1 tablespoon extra-virgin olive oil

2 teaspoons sugar

½ teaspoon fine sea salt

12 medium or large raw shrimp (about 1 pound/455 g), peeled and deveined, tails left on

MANGO SALSA

Makes about 1 cup (150 g)

1 ripe mango, peeled, pitted, and diced

2 tablespoons finely chopped red onion

¼ to ½ small jalapeño, seeded and minced

¼ cup (5 g) fresh cilantro leaves, chopped

2 tablespoons fresh lime juice

Fine sea salt

STORE-BOUGHT COMPONENTS

Salty thick-cut tortilla chips

1 ripe avocado, sliced into bite-size pieces

½ lime

Pickle the shrimp: Bring a small pot of generously salted water to a boil. While it heats up, make the pickling liquid by combining the ice cubes, garlic, chile, vinegar, lemon juice, oil, sugar, and salt in a large jar. Lower the shrimp into the boiling water and cook just until they're pink and opaque, about 2 minutes. Use a slotted spoon to transfer the cooked shrimp to the pickling liquid. Let the shrimp cool in the jar, tossing occasionally, for at least 15 minutes and up to 24 hours in the refrigerator.

Make the mango salad: Just before you're ready to serve the shrimp, stir together the mango, onion, jalapeño, cilantro, and lime juice, then season with salt to taste.

Assemble: Drain off most of the pickled shrimp brine and place the jar directly on a board (with a small bowl for the discarded shrimp tails). Serve the salsa in its own small jar or bowl, with the tortilla chips and sliced avocado alongside. Squeeze the lime juice over the avocado to keep it from turning brown and sprinkle with a pinch of salt.

Toothpicks are really fun and helpful with this board. They're great for spearing a piece of avocado or for fishing a pickled shrimp out of the jar.

vegetable-
focused

mostly-vegetables chicken salad crostini

radish-cucumber-chicken salad	+	leafy green tangle	+	country-style bread	+	grapes

Serves 2 to 4 ▪ This chicken salad is held together with just enough creamy aioli and brightened up with the addition of preserved lemon, a salty and flavorful ingredient that you can find in the condiments section of your grocery store. (Chopped preserved lemon peel is wonderful stirred into rice, and the brine left behind in the jar makes the best addition to a Bloody Mary.)

CHICKEN SALAD

Makes about 2 cups (400 g)

6 ounces (170 g) roasted chicken (homemade or store-bought), chopped

3 radishes, very thinly sliced

1 Persian cucumber, very thinly sliced

¼ cup plus 2 tablespoons (90 ml) Aioli (page 91)

¼ preserved lemon (see headnote)

Fine sea salt

Freshly ground black pepper

STORE-BOUGHT COMPONENTS

3 or 4 slices of country-style bread (like rustic sourdough)

2 handfuls of arugula or other leafy green

½ lemon

8 ounces (225 g) seedless red or green grapes

Make the chicken salad: In a large bowl, combine the roasted chicken, radishes, cucumber, and aioli. To prepare the preserved lemon, use a small knife to remove and discard the squishy inside part, then finely chop the peel and add it to the bowl. (If you can't find preserved lemon, finely grate the zest from a regular lemon and add it along with a big pinch of salt.) Gently mix all the ingredients together, then taste and season with salt and pepper. Transfer the chicken salad to a small serving bowl.

Assemble: Place the bowl of chicken salad on one side of the board and set a serving spoon in it. Toast the bread, if you want, cut it into 2-inch (5 cm) sections on the diagonal, and arrange it next to the chicken salad. Place the arugula greens nearby, squeeze a little lemon juice over them, and season with salt and pepper. You can use kitchen shears to snip the grapes into smaller clusters, if you prefer, before setting them on the board.

Spread some chicken salad on a piece of toasted bread and top with a tangle of leafy greens for the perfect bite.

lebanese lunch

Serves 4 to 6 • This vegetarian board is ideal for a leisurely meal. All the dipping and swooping of the warm pita in the lemony hummus feels indulgent and satisfying. The muhammara, a thickened roasted pepper sauce, spread over the pita is wonderful when topped with the tangy, creamy marinated cheese.

HUMMUS

Makes about 1½ cups (370 g)

1 garlic clove, minced

¼ cup (60 ml) fresh lemon juice

Fine sea salt

1 (15-ounce/425 g) can of chickpeas, drained and rinsed

1 tablespoon tahini

2 to 3 tablespoons ice water

Freshly ground black pepper

Extra-virgin olive oil, to drizzle

Za'atar, to sprinkle (optional but highly recommended)

MUHAMMARA

Makes 1¼ cups (290 g)

¼ cup (30 g) walnuts

1 (8-ounce/225g) jar of roasted peppers, drained and rinsed

2 tablespoons dried plain breadcrumbs

1 tablespoon extra-virgin olive oil

1 tablespoon fresh lemon juice

1 tablespoon pomegranate molasses, plus more to drizzle

½ teaspoon smoked paprika (sweet or hot)

¼ teaspoon chile flakes

¼ teaspoon cumin seeds

¼ teaspoon fine sea salt

Freshly ground black pepper

(ingredients continue on next page)

STORE-BOUGHT COMPONENTS

Stack of pita bread, warmed, or whole-wheat sesame crackers

Labne or Greek yogurt (not pictured)

Radishes, sliced or cut into wedges for dipping

Sheep or goat cheese marinated in olive oil, preferably Meredith Dairy or Laura Chenel

Make the hummus: In a food processor, combine the garlic, lemon juice, and ½ teaspoon of salt. Let rest for at least 5 minutes so the flavor of the garlic mellows. Add the chickpeas and tahini and blend to a smooth paste. While the machine is spinning, drizzle in 2 tablespoons of ice water. Stop the machine, scrape down the sides, and taste the hummus. Season with a little more salt and pepper. If you'd like it to be looser, mix in another 1 tablespoon of ice water. Blend until super creamy. Spoon the hummus into a small serving bowl. Drizzle with olive oil and sprinkle with za'atar, if using.

Make the muhammara: Toast the walnuts in a dry skillet over medium heat, stirring often, until fragrant and browned in some places, about 6 minutes. Clean the food processor and use it to blend the toasted walnuts and all the other muhammara ingredients until completely smooth. Taste and season with more salt and black pepper plus a little extra chile flakes, if you'd like it to be spicier. Transfer to another small serving bowl and drizzle with pomegranate molasses.

Assemble: Serve the pita (whole or cut into wedges) on the board alongside the bowls of hummus and muhammara. Spoon some labne into another small bowl and season with a pinch of salt and several grinds of pepper. Place the radishes and marinated cheese on the board as well.

from the garden, see page 56

from the garden

beet dip with pine nut crunch + lemon-basil white bean dip + quick pickles + honeyed ricotta

+ prosciutto and melon + seeded crackers

Serves 8 to 10 • Inspired by the bounty of a garden, this board features not one but two tasty dips for quick-pickled cucumbers and carrots (or any favorite vegetables). For a vegan version of the beet dip, leave out the sour cream.

BEET DIP

Makes about 2 cups (455 g)

4 medium beets (about 1 pound/455 g), scrubbed and tops trimmed

¼ cup (60 ml) plus 2 tablespoons extra-virgin olive oil, plus more to drizzle

Fine sea salt

Freshly ground black pepper

1 garlic clove

2 tablespoons red wine vinegar

½ cup (115 g) sour cream or labne or plain whole-milk yogurt

2 tablespoons pine nuts

1 tablespoon white sesame seeds

¼ teaspoon chile flakes

QUICK PICKLES

1 cup (240 ml) rice vinegar, apple cider vinegar, or white wine vinegar

1 cup (240 ml) water

2 teaspoons sugar

1 teaspoon fine sea salt

4 garlic cloves, halved

6 sprigs of thyme

1 bay leaf

1 small dried hot chile, such as chile de árbol (optional)

6 black peppercorns

4 small carrots, peeled and halved lengthwise

1 or 2 Persian cucumbers, cut into spears

LEMON-BASIL WHITE BEAN DIP

Makes about 1⅓ cups (320 g)

1 (15-ounce/425 g) can of cannellini or other white beans, drained and rinsed

⅓ cup (7 g) fresh basil leaves

Finely grated zest of 1 lemon

2 tablespoons lemon juice

2 tablespoons extra-virgin olive oil

½ teaspoon fine sea salt

1 tablespoon hot water

STORE-BOUGHT COMPONENTS

1 (12-ounce/340 g) basket ricotta

1 handful of tender herbs like basil, dill, flat-leaf parsley, or a combination

2 to 3 tablespoons honey

12 ounces (340 g) thinly sliced prosciutto

1 small cantaloupe, cut into thin wedges

Seeded crackers

Start the beet dip: Heat the oven to 425°F (220°C).

Place the beets on a baking sheet, drizzle with olive oil, and season with a few pinches each of salt and pepper. Roast the beets until completely tender all the way through when poked with a fork, about 1 hour. Remove the beets from the oven and let them cool.

Make the quick pickles: While the beets are roasting, in a small saucepan, combine the vinegar, water, sugar, salt, garlic, thyme, bay leaf, chile, and peppercorns. Bring to a boil. Add the carrots to the pot and cook for 1 minute, then add the cucumber spears and immediately remove the pot from the heat. Let the pickles cool to room temperature in their brine. The pickles can be made ahead and stored in their brine in an airtight container in the refrigerator for up to 3 weeks.

Make the white bean dip: In a food processor, combine the beans, basil, lemon zest, lemon juice, olive oil, and salt. Blend until puréed. With the food processor running, slowly drizzle in the water and blend until smooth and creamy. Transfer the white bean dip to a serving bowl.

Finish the beet dip: Once the beets are cool enough to handle, peel them and discard the peels. Chop the peeled beets into 2-inch (5 cm) pieces and place them in a food processor. Add the garlic, vinegar, ¼ cup (60 ml) of the olive oil, ½ teaspoon of salt, and a not-at-all-shy amount of pepper (about 6 grinds of the pepper mill). Blend until smooth. Transfer the beet dip to a shallow serving bowl. Add the sour cream in big spoonfuls on top of the beet dip and use a small spoon to swirl the two together. Just a few swirls are all it takes to look beautiful; try to keep a striking contrast between the beets and the sour cream.

In a small skillet, warm the remaining 2 tablespoons oil over medium heat. Add the pine nuts, sesame seeds, and chile flakes.

Cook, stirring often, until the nuts and seeds are toasted and golden brown, about 3 minutes. Spoon over the beet dip.

Assemble: Place the two dips on a large platter. The quick pickles can be served without their brine directly on the board. Invert the basket ricotta onto a small plate. Tear or chop the herbs into small pieces and scatter them over the ricotta. Drizzle the honey, letting it drip down the sides of the cheese. Arrange the prosciutto, cantaloupe, and crackers around everything.

when in rome

fresh mozzarella and cherry tomato bites   +   pistachio pesto   +   olive tapenade   +   focaccia

Serves 4 to 6 • Pistachio pesto, which is a little greener than the classic pine nut version, is a lovely variation to try. Here it's served alongside olive tapenade as dipping options for fresh mozzarella and tomato bites.

PISTACHIO PESTO

Makes about ⅔ cup (165 g)

1¼ cups (25 g) fresh basil leaves

⅓ cup (45 g) pistachios, toasted

1 garlic clove

Finely grated zest from ½ lemon

1 tablespoon fresh lemon juice

½ teaspoon fine sea salt

⅓ cup (80 ml) extra-virgin olive oil

Freshly ground black pepper

OLIVE TAPENADE

Makes about ⅔ cup (140 g)

½ cup (55 g) pitted Niçoise olives

1 garlic clove, finely chopped

1 anchovy fillet, rinsed

Finely grated zest from ½ lemon

1 tablespoon fresh lemon juice

¼ cup (60 ml) extra-virgin olive oil

Freshly ground black pepper

MOZZARELLA AND CHERRY TOMATO BITES

12 cherry tomatoes, halved

9 ounces (255 g) bite-size balls of fresh mozzarella (or large balls cut into ¾-inch/2 cm pieces)

Flaky sea salt

Freshly ground black pepper

STORE-BOUGHT COMPONENTS

Focaccia, cut into bite-size squares

Make the pesto: Use a food processor to blend the basil, pistachios, garlic, lemon zest, lemon juice, and salt until finely chopped. Pour in the olive oil all at once and blend until mostly smooth. Taste and season with more salt and pepper. Spoon the pesto into a small serving bowl.

Make the tapenade: Clean the food processor and use it to pulse the olives, garlic, anchovy, lemon zest, and lemon juice just until the olives are coarsely chopped. Pour in the olive oil all at once and blend until the oil is just incorporated and the olives are finely ground but not yet a smooth paste. (Alternatively, for a more rustic tapenade, finely chop the olives, garlic, and anchovy and stir in the lemon zest, lemon juice, and oil.) Taste and season with pepper; the olives are usually salty enough that tapenade doesn't need additional salt. Spoon the tapenade into a small serving bowl.

Make the mozzarella and tomato bites: Stack a cherry tomato half on top of a piece of cheese and skewer the two together with a toothpick.

Assemble: Arrange the tomato and mozzarella bites on a serving board and season them with flaky salt and pepper. Serve with the bowls of pesto and tapenade for dipping, and place the focaccia squares alongside.

green goddess

"grilled" vegetables + green goddess sauce + seven-minute eggs + flatbread crackers

Serves 4 to 6 • Vegetables cooked over an open flame are a simple delight, but you don't really need a grill for this recipe—you can achieve the same effect by using a smoking-hot cast-iron skillet. The key is to not flip the vegetables too often. They'll take on beautiful char marks and even taste a little smoky. Use any vegetables you like; you'll need about 1 pound (455 g) total.

GREEN GODDESS SAUCE

Makes 1 cup (240 ml)

¾ cup (15 g) fresh parsley leaves

¾ cup (15 g) fresh basil leaves

1 tablespoon fresh tarragon leaves

1 tablespoon chopped chives

2 anchovy fillets, rinsed

2 tablespoons fresh lemon juice

¼ teaspoon fine sea salt

⅔ cup (160 g) crème fraîche

Freshly ground black pepper

VEGETABLES

8 ounces (225 g) shishito or padrón peppers

3 small summer squash, thinly sliced lengthwise or cut into 1-inch (2.5 cm) wedges

2 tablespoons extra-virgin olive oil

½ teaspoon fine sea salt

¼ teaspoon freshly ground black pepper

4 Seven-Minute Eggs (page 32), peeled and halved lengthwise (not pictured)

STORE-BOUGHT COMPONENTS

Flatbread-style crackers (not pictured)

Make the green goddess: Use a food processor to blend the parsley, basil, tarragon, chives, anchovies, lemon juice, and salt until very finely chopped. Transfer the herb mixture to a bowl and stir in the crème fraîche. Taste and season with plenty of pepper and more salt if needed. Cover and store in the refrigerator until ready to serve, up to 3 days.

"Grill" the vegetables: Heat a cast-iron skillet over medium-high heat for 5 minutes. While it heats up, drizzle the peppers and squash with the olive oil, and season them with the salt and pepper. Working in batches so as not to crowd the pan, place the vegetables in the skillet and cook, without stirring, until browned on the bottom side. Flip and cook on the other side until browned and just tender, about 10 minutes total.

Assemble: Spread the green goddess across a large serving platter and arrange the grilled vegetables on top of the sauce. Nestle the eggs among the grilled vegetables. (Alternatively, you could serve the green goddess in a bowl for dipping, with the vegetables and eggs arranged around it on the board.) Serve the flatbread crackers on the side.

vegan rainbow, see page 68

vegan rainbow

vegan rainbow rolls + peanut dipping sauce + jicama + pineapple + vegetable chips

Serves 4 to 6 • These rainbow rolls are a vegan take on the classic shrimp-and-pork version. They are filled with colorful vegetables and herbs plus pressed tofu, which is exactly what it sounds like. If you can't find pressed tofu, use regular extra-firm tofu or avocado.

RAINBOW ROLLS

Makes 8

8 (9-inch/23 cm) rice-paper rounds

¼ small head of purple cabbage, sliced as thinly as possible

1 small red bell pepper, stemmed, seeded, and cut into matchsticks

1 carrot, peeled and cut into matchsticks

2 Persian cucumbers, sliced into matchsticks, or ⅓ English cucumber, peeled, seeded, and sliced into matchsticks

4 ounces (115 g) pressed tofu, cut into matchsticks

1 handful fresh Thai basil or regular basil leaves

1 handful fresh mint leaves

PEANUT SAUCE

Makes 1 cup (240 ml)

2 garlic cloves

2 tablespoons rice vinegar

½ cup (135 g) smooth or crunchy peanut butter

2 tablespoons soy sauce or tamari

2 tablespoons light or dark brown sugar

4 teaspoons sesame oil

2 to 4 tablespoons (30 to 60 ml) ice water

STORE-BOUGHT COMPONENTS

Jicama, peeled and cut into batons

Pineapple, cut into small wedges

Vegetable chips

Make the rainbow rolls: First make sure all the fillings are ready to go—peeled, chopped, and sliced—and neatly arranged for ease of assembly. Fill a wide sauté pan with hot water from the tap. Working with one rice-paper round at a time, soak it in the hot water until it's pliable, 5 to 20 seconds. Remove the round from the water and lay it flat on a clean work surface. Keep in mind that you have enough filling for about 8 rolls, and portion it out accordingly. Arrange some cabbage, a few matchsticks of the vegetables and tofu, and a few herb leaves on the bottom one-third of the round, leaving about 1 inch (2.5 cm) of open rice paper at the bottom edge. Fold in the left and right sides of the rice-paper round, then lift the bottom edge up and over the filling. Tightly roll the rice paper to form a compact cylinder. Repeat with the remaining rice-paper rounds and fillings. The rolls can be made ahead and refrigerated, covered with a clean damp tea towel, for up to 2 hours.

Make the peanut sauce: Using a mortar and pestle or the side of a large knife, crush the garlic to a paste. Transfer the garlic paste to a medium bowl and pour in the vinegar. Let it rest for a few minutes so the flavor of the garlic mellows. Whisk in the peanut butter, soy sauce, brown sugar, sesame oil, and 2 tablespoons of ice water. The sauce should be thick but dippable. If you'd like the sauce to be a little looser, whisk in more water, 1 tablespoon at a time. Spoon the peanut sauce into a small serving bowl.

Assemble: Just before serving, cut the rainbow rolls into thirds and arrange them on a board. Serve the bowl of peanut dipping sauce on the side along with the jicama, pineapple, and vegetable chips.

DIY hoagie bar

cured meats	+	provolone	+	spicy pepper mayonnaise	+	iceberg slaw	+	sesame loaf

Serves 4 to 6 • The beauty of a DIY hoagie bar is that everyone gets to make their own sandwich exactly how they like it. I'll take mine with extra iceberg slaw and spicy pepper mayonnaise, please! Make-your-own hoagies are perfect for gatherings of all kinds, especially game-day parties.

SPICY PEPPER MAYONNAISE

Makes about ½ cup (115 g)

5 whole (about 1 ounce/30 g) hot chile peppers in oil (such as Calabrian cherry peppers), stemmed and finely chopped, plus a few extra whole peppers, for garnish

½ cup (115 g) mayonnaise

Fine sea salt

Freshly ground black pepper

ICEBERG SLAW

1 small head (about 1 pound/455 g) of iceberg lettuce

4 teaspoons red wine vinegar

4 teaspoons extra-virgin olive oil

2 teaspoons dried oregano

½ teaspoon fine sea salt

Freshly ground black pepper

STORE-BOUGHT COMPONENTS

1 (16-inch/40 cm) loaf of soft Italian bread with sesame seeds

4 ounces (115 g) thinly sliced mortadella

4 ounces (115 g) thinly sliced soppressata

4 ounces (115 g) thinly sliced Genoa salami

4 ounces (115 g) sliced provolone

½ red onion, thinly sliced

2 ripe tomatoes, sliced

Ridged salt-and-pepper potato chips

Make the spicy pepper mayonnaise: In a small serving bowl, stir together the chopped peppers and mayonnaise. Season with a pinch of salt and several grinds of black pepper. Cover and store the mayonnaise in the refrigerator until you're ready to serve, up to 3 days.

Make the iceberg slaw: Just before serving, remove the core and any bruised outer leaves from the head of lettuce. Thinly slice the lettuce and place it in a medium serving bowl. Add the vinegar, olive oil, oregano, salt, and plenty of pepper. Toss well.

Assemble: Place the bowls of spicy pepper mayonnaise and iceberg slaw on a board, with serving utensils for each. Cut the sesame loaf in half lengthwise and then crosswise into 4 or 6 pieces. Arrange the bread, mortadella, soppressata, salami, provolone, red onion, tomatoes, and extra whole peppers next to the mayonnaise and slaw. Serve the chips alongside in a bowl.

tiny baked potato poppers

baked new potatoes	+	real bacon bits	+	garlic-chive butter	+	sour cream

Serves 4 to 6 • Homemade bacon bits taste way better than the store-bought kind. Plus, cooking the bacon gives you a few spoonfuls of fat that can be drizzled over the potatoes before they go into the oven, which really adds to the flavor of these tiny poppers.

BACON BITS

4 slices of bacon (about 4 ounces/ 115 g total)

BAKED POTATOES

12 to 18 small red, yellow, or purple potatoes (about 1½ pounds/680 g total)

Fine sea salt

Freshly ground black pepper

GARLIC-CHIVE BUTTER

1 garlic clove

1 tablespoon finely chopped chives

Fine sea salt

¼ cup (½ stick/55 g) unsalted butter, at room temperature

STORE-BOUGHT COMPONENTS

Sour cream

Shredded cheddar cheese

Green onions, white and green parts thinly sliced

Flaky sea salt

Freshly ground black pepper

Make the bacon bits: Heat the oven to 425°F (220°C). Line a plate with paper towels or a clean brown paper bag and set aside.

In a large skillet, cook the bacon over medium heat, stirring occasionally, until browned and crispy, 8 to 10 minutes. Use tongs to transfer the bacon to the prepared plate to drain, reserving the fat in the skillet. Let the bacon cool slightly, then transfer it to a cutting board and chop it into bits.

Bake the potatoes: Place the potatoes on a rimmed baking sheet. Spoon 1 tablespoon of bacon fat over the potatoes and sprinkle with a few pinches each of fine salt and pepper. Mix the potatoes around on the baking sheet to evenly coat them in the seasoning. Bake until the potatoes are browned on the outside and fluffy inside, 25 to 30 minutes. When the potatoes are done, set them aside until ready to serve, but make sure not to cut into the potatoes until right before you eat them, so they stay piping hot.

Make the garlic-chive butter: While the potatoes are baking, using a mortar and pestle or the side of a large knife, crush the garlic into a paste. In a small bowl, stir the garlic paste, chives, and 2 big pinches of fine salt into the softened butter.

Assemble: On a serving platter, arrange the potatoes with a knife alongside for cutting them. Serve the bacon bits, garlic-chive butter, sour cream, cheddar cheese, and green onions all in their own bowls, plus two more tiny bowls of flaky salt and pepper. Napkins are necessary here!

chips and crispy chickpeas

pita chips	+	crispy chickpeas	+	harissa-sumac sauce	+	manouri cheese	+	black olives

Serves 2 to 4 • Manouri is a mild semisoft cheese that tastes like fresh milk. It doesn't melt when heated, but that actually makes it ideal for scooping up with a crisp baked pita chip. This board also has a flame-colored sauce that cloaks the chips and hidden pockets of oil-cured black olives. Use a baking dish that can go straight from oven to table, then dig in!

CRISPY CHICKPEAS

1 (15-ounce/425 g) can of chickpeas, drained and rinsed

2 tablespoons extra-virgin olive oil

¼ teaspoon fine sea salt

Freshly ground black pepper

HARISSA-SUMAC SAUCE

Makes about ½ cup (120 ml)

2 tablespoons harissa paste

2 tablespoons sherry vinegar or red wine vinegar

2 tablespoons extra-virgin olive oil

2 teaspoons sumac

STORE-BOUGHT COMPONENTS

1 (7-ounce/200 g) bag of pita chips

3 ounces (85 g) manouri cheese, thinly sliced

¼ cup (30 g) pitted oil-cured black olives, coarsely chopped

2 sprigs of mint, stemmed

2 sprigs of flat-leaf parsley, stemmed

Make the crispy chickpeas: Heat the oven to 400°F (200°C).

On a quarter-sheet pan or small rimmed baking sheet, spread out the chickpeas, drizzle them with the oil, and season with the salt and several grinds of pepper. Mix well. Roast, stirring once or twice, until golden brown and crispy, about 20 minutes. When the chickpeas are done roasting, transfer them to a bowl and keep the oven on. Set aside the baking sheet to use again once everything has been assembled.

Make the harissa-sumac sauce: In a small bowl, stir together the harissa, vinegar, olive oil, and sumac.

Assemble: Place the pita chips on the baking sheet used for the chickpeas. Tuck the manouri cheese slices among the chips. Scatter the olives and crispy chickpeas on top, and spoon the harissa-sumac sauce over all. Bake until everything is hot and the cheese has softened, about 10 minutes.

Garnish with the mint and parsley. Serve right away on the baking sheet.

onigiri

steamed rice	+	spicy tuna filling	+	nori	+	shichimi togarashi	+	edamame

Serves 4 to 8 • Onigiri are snackable, portable Japanese rice triangles wrapped in nori and filled with salty or sour ingredients like pickled plum. This version is filled with spicy tuna. The heat comes from shichimi togarashi, a seasoning blend of seven ingredients, including various ground chile peppers and orange peel. To keep the crackly crisp texture of the nori, make sure to wait to wrap it around the rice until right before eating.

STEAMED RICE

4 cups (960 ml) water

2 cups (400 g) short-grain white rice, rinsed

1 teaspoon fine sea salt, plus more for shaping the triangles

SPICY TUNA FILLING

1 (5-ounce/140 g) can of albacore or yellowfin tuna in extra-virgin olive oil, drained

2 tablespoons mayonnaise

1 teaspoon rice vinegar

¾ teaspoon shichimi togarashi, plus more to serve

Fine sea salt

1 green onion, white and green parts, very thinly sliced

STORE-BOUGHT COMPONENTS

4 sheets toasted nori

3 tablespoons white and/or black sesame seeds

Soy sauce or tamari

8 ounces (225 g) edamame in the pod

Make the steamed rice: In a medium saucepan, bring the water to a boil. Add the rice and salt. Lower the heat to medium-low, cover the pot, and cook for 18 minutes. Remove the lid and fluff the rice with a fork. Let cool until just slightly warm.

Make the spicy tuna filling: In a small bowl, mix together the tuna, mayonnaise, vinegar, shichimi togarashi, a pinch of salt, and most of the green onion (save a few slices for garnishing) until well combined.

To shape the onigiri, fill a small bowl with lightly salted warm water. Lightly wet your hands with the water (this helps prevent the rice from sticking to your hands), then scoop up a palm-size amount of the steamed rice, about one-eighth of the total rice. Use your hands to shape the rice into a triangle, make an indentation in the center of it, and fill it with 1 tablespoon of the spicy tuna mixture. Pinch and mold the rice to enclose the filling, adding a little more rice if needed to completely cover the filling. Repeat with the remaining rice and spicy tuna to create 8 onigiri.

Assemble: Place the rice triangles on a serving board. Use clean kitchen shears to cut each sheet of nori in half. Arrange the nori next to the triangles so that everyone can wrap the nori around the rice right before eating, to keep the nori crisp. Serve the sesame seeds, extra shichimi togarashi, and soy sauce in individual small bowls for sprinkling and dipping. Place the edamame directly on the board as well and set an empty bowl alongside for the pods.

summertime bagna cauda, see page 86

summertime bagna cauda

Parmigiano twists + garlic-anchovy dipping sauce + balsamic vinegar dip + summer vegetables + Italian cheeses

Serves 8 to 10 • Bagna cauda, which means "warm bath" in Italian, is a super-flavorful sauce for garlic lovers. This recipe is not at all traditional because bagna cauda is usually served during the cold months of winter. However, summer vegetables taste wonderful dipped into the sauce, too. Any leftover twists can be frozen in an airtight container and reheated for a few minutes in a hot oven when you need a little snack.

GARLIC-ANCHOVY SAUCE

Makes about 1½ cups (360 ml)

10 garlic cloves

1 cup (240 ml) extra-virgin olive oil

¼ cup (½ stick/55 g) unsalted butter

12 anchovy fillets, rinsed

PARMIGIANO TWISTS

Makes 24

1½ cups (6 ounces/170 g) finely grated Parmigiano-Reggiano cheese

1½ teaspoons dried oregano

¼ teaspoon chile flakes

¾ teaspoon flaky sea salt

¼ teaspoon freshly ground black pepper

All-purpose flour, for dusting

2 sheets (from one 17.3-ounce/490g package) frozen puff pastry, defrosted

Extra-virgin olive oil

BALSAMIC VINEGAR DIP	STORE-BOUGHT COMPONENTS	2 cups (130 g) sugar snap peas
¼ cup (60 ml) extra-virgin olive oil	1 basket of cherry tomatoes	1 large wedge of Fontina cheese
1 tablespoon balsamic vinegar	4 lemon cucumbers, cut into wedges, or 1 English cucumber, cut into two-bite sticks	7 ounces (200 g) La Tur cheese or other soft Italian cheese
Freshly ground black pepper	4 small sweet peppers (like bell peppers), stemmed, seeded, and sliced into strips	1 large wedge of gorgonzola dolce or regular gorgonzola cheese

Make the garlic-anchovy sauce: Thinly slice half of the garlic cloves and mince the other half. The two different textures will be twice as appealing in the finished sauce than if it was made with just one. In a small saucepan, place both the sliced and minced garlic with the olive oil, butter, and anchovies. Cook over very low heat until the garlic is soft and fragrant but not at all browned and the anchovies have dissolved into the oil and butter, 20 to 25 minutes. Remove from the heat and set aside.

Make the Parmigiano twists: While the sauce cooks, you can get started on the twists. Heat the oven to 400°F (200°C). Line 2 baking sheets with parchment paper.

On a large plate, mix together the Parmigiano, oregano, chile flakes, flaky salt, and pepper. On a lightly floured surface, roll out each sheet of puff pastry into a 9-inch (23 cm) square. Cut the square into 12 equal strips, each about ¾ inch (2 cm) wide. Brush the strips with olive oil on one side, then gently lift one strip at a time from the work surface and press the oily side into the cheese mixture. Twist a strip by holding each end with one hand and rotating a few times to create a corkscrew shape. Place it on one of the prepared baking sheets and repeat with the other strips. Bake, switching the position of the baking sheets halfway through, until the twists are golden brown and crispy, about 12 minutes. Let the twists cool slightly on the baking sheets.

Make the balsamic vinegar dip: Pour the olive oil into a small serving dish. Add the balsamic and sprinkle in some pepper.

Assemble: Transfer the garlic-anchovy dipping sauce to a small serving dish and set it on a platter along with the balsamic dip. The garlic-anchovy sauce tastes best when it's warm, so if you're having a party, you can top up the dish with hot sauce once or twice. Arrange the cherry tomatoes, cucumbers, sweet peppers, and sugar snap peas around the two dipping sauces. Serve the Parmigiano twists and Italian cheeses alongside (with a small serving knife for each cheese).

le grand aioli

aioli	+	haricots verts	+	boiled potatoes	+	Niçoise olives	+	shrimp	+	seven-minute eggs

Serves 4 • This traditional French platter is all about the aioli, which is definitely worth making at home frequently because it is so delicious spread on sandwiches, served as a dip for oven fries, and mixed into chicken salad (see page 49). Once you've made the aioli, the rest of the dish comes together easily. It's just a matter of gathering components, with very little cooking involved.

AIOLI

Makes about ¾ cup (180 ml)

2 or 3 small garlic cloves

Fine sea salt

1 egg yolk

¾ cup (180 ml) extra-virgin olive oil

½ lemon

COOKED VEGETABLES AND SHRIMP

Fine sea salt

4 small or 10 marble-size (about 7 ounces/200 g) red or yellow potatoes, cut into halves if large

4 ounces (115 g) haricots verts, stem ends trimmed but you can leave their little tails

12 medium or large raw shrimp (about 1 pound/455 g), peeled and deveined, tails left on

4 Seven-Minute Eggs (page 32), peeled and halved

STORE-BOUGHT COMPONENTS

¼ cup (30 g) Niçoise olives or other olives

2 Belgian endives, separated into individual leaves

1 baguette, sliced (optional)

Make the aioli: Using a mortar and pestle or the side of a large knife, crush the garlic and 2 or 3 pinches of salt into a smooth paste. In a medium bowl, whisk the egg yolk to break it up. While whisking continuously, add a few drops of the olive oil. Whisk until fully incorporated, then add a few more drops of oil. Continue whisking and adding the oil by the drop until the mixture thickens, looks sticky, and pulls away from the sides of the bowl. While whisking continuously, add a little more oil, this time in a very thin and slow stream. Once you've added somewhere between one-third and one-half the total oil, squeeze in a little lemon juice to thin the aioli. Add the remaining oil, still in a very thin and slow stream while whisking continuously. The aioli should be as thick as mayonnaise. If it's thin and watery, it broke—whoops! Don't worry, this happens to the best of us, and you can easily fix broken aioli. Start with a fresh egg yolk in a clean bowl. Follow the recipe as outlined above, but instead of adding oil to the egg yolk, add the broken aioli mixture (first drop by drop and then in a very thin and slow stream) while whisking continuously. I find it most helpful to transfer the broken aioli mixture to a liquid measuring cup or something with a pour spout.

Stir the garlic paste into the aioli. Taste and adjust the seasoning, adding more salt and lemon juice if you'd like. Transfer the aioli to a small serving bowl or store in an airtight container in the refrigerator for up to 2 days.

Cook the vegetables and then the shrimp: Bring a medium saucepan of generously salted water to a boil. Add the potatoes and cook until they are tender when poked with a fork, about

15 minutes. Use a slotted spoon to transfer the boiled potatoes to a plate.

To the same pot of boiling water, add the haricots verts. Cook until bright green and tender but still a little crunchy, about 1½ minutes. Use a slotted spoon to transfer the beans to a colander and rinse with cold water.

Finally, cook the shrimp by carefully lowering them into the boiling water and cooking just until they're pink and opaque, about 2 minutes. Use a slotted spoon to transfer the shrimp to one side of a serving platter.

Assemble: Place the bowl of aioli next to the shrimp on the platter, just off-center. Arrange the cooked vegetables, eggs, olives, endive leaves, and baguette slices (if using) around the shrimp and aioli in separate little areas on the platter.

cocktail
parties

new year's eve, see page 98

new year's eve

bite-size latkes + homemade applesauce + sour cream + smoked salmon + sliced cucumber + dill

Serves 8 to 10 One-bite latkes are the ideal size for a party board, and their dimensions also make them crispier than regular-size ones. Good-quality store-bought applesauce will do the trick, but homemade applesauce takes only about twenty minutes to cook, and you can customize the sweetness to your liking.

APPLESAUCE

Makes about 2 cups (490 g)

4 apples (about 1¾ pounds/795 g), like Fuji, Pink Lady, or Gravenstein, peeled, cored, and chopped

¾ cup (180 ml) apple juice or water

4 tablespoons (50 g) sugar

1 strip of lemon peel (use a vegetable peeler to cut the strip)

½ teaspoon ground cinnamon

Fine sea salt

LATKES

Makes about 36

4 russet potatoes (about 2 pounds/900 g)

2 teaspoons fine sea salt

½ small yellow onion, very finely chopped

2 large eggs

½ teaspoon freshly ground black pepper

2 tablespoons finely chopped dill, plus a few whole sprigs for garnish

½ cup (120 ml) extra-virgin olive oil

STORE-BOUGHT COMPONENTS

1 cup (225 g) sour cream

1 small jar of capers, drained and rinsed

1 large English cucumber or 3 small Persian cucumbers, sliced

8 ounces (225 g) thinly sliced smoked salmon

Make the applesauce: In a medium saucepan, combine the apples, apple juice, 2 tablespoons of the sugar, the lemon peel, cinnamon, and a pinch of salt. Bring to a boil, then cover the pan and lower the heat to medium-low. Cook, stirring occasionally, until the apples are very soft, 15 to 20 minutes. Remove from the heat, discard the lemon peel, and use a potato masher to mash the apples until mostly smooth. (Alternatively, for super-smooth applesauce, use a blender or food processor to purée the cooked apples.) Taste and season with the remaining 2 tablespoons sugar if you'd like the applesauce to be sweeter. Allow the applesauce to cool before serving. The applesauce can be stored in an airtight container in the refrigerator for up to 10 days.

Make the latkes: Peel and coarsely grate the potatoes on a box grater. In a medium bowl, toss the grated potato with the salt and let rest for a few minutes. Gather the salted, grated potato in a fine-mesh nut milk bag or cheesecloth and squeeze the mixture while holding it over a clean, small bowl, wringing out all the moisture and collecting the liquid in the bowl. (You can also do this by hand without a cloth, working in batches and squeezing fist-size amounts of grated potato.) Once squeezed, return the grated potato to the medium bowl. Let the liquid in the small bowl rest for about 5 minutes, until an opaque white layer of starch settles on the bottom of the bowl. Carefully pour off and discard the clear liquid so that you are left with only the starch in the bowl. Stir the starch into the grated potatoes along with the onion, eggs, pepper, and chopped dill.

Line a plate with paper towels or a clean brown paper bag and set aside. In a large cast-iron skillet, heat ¼ cup (60 ml) of the oil over medium-high heat for 1 minute. Working in batches so as not to crowd the pan, spoon about 1 tablespoon of the potato mixture per latke into the skillet, and flatten the latke with a spatula. Lower the heat to medium and cook until the latkes are golden brown on the bottom side, about 5 minutes. Flip and cook until the other side is golden brown, another 3 minutes or so. Transfer to the prepared plate to drain. Repeat to cook the remaining latkes, adding oil to the pan as needed between batches. The second and subsequent batches might cook a little faster than the first, so keep a close eye on the color of the latkes.

Assemble: Serve the hot latkes on a large platter with small bowls of applesauce, sour cream, and capers. Arrange the sliced cucumber and smoked salmon alongside, and garnish with the whole dill sprigs.

HOW TO MAKE AHEAD

Latkes can be kept warm in a single layer on a baking sheet (no paper towels!) in a 200°F (90°C) oven for up to 1 hour. They can also be cooked ahead, stored in the refrigerator for a day or two, and reheated in a single layer on a baking sheet in a 350°F (180°C) oven until crisp, about 10 minutes.

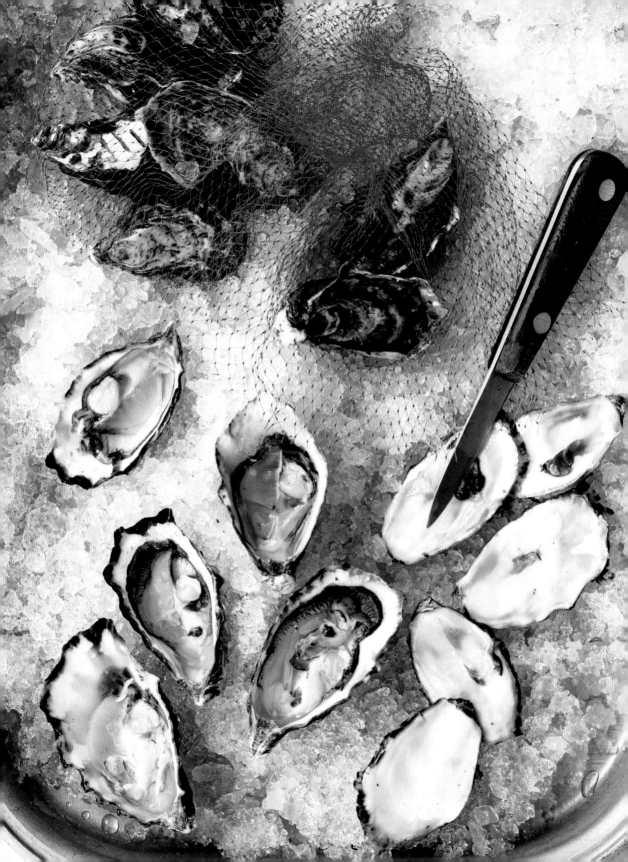

the 007

oysters on
the half shell
+
vodka mignonette
sauce
+
lemony
frisée
+
buttered
toast

Serves 2 to 4 • This platter, with its dozen oysters and accoutrements, is the kind of feast that James Bond would love. A splash of vodka gives the mignonette sauce a surprising pop. Champagne vinegar seems appropriate in the sauce as well, although you can substitute any white wine vinegar you have on hand. Keeping the oysters cold on a bed of crushed ice is important. If you don't want to make crushed ice (a food processor will do it, but the process isn't a quiet one!), ask the person who sells you the oysters for a bag of clean crushed ice.

VODKA MIGNONETTE SAUCE

Makes 6 tablespoons (90 ml)

2 tablespoons very finely chopped shallot

2 tablespoons Champagne vinegar or white wine vinegar

2 tablespoons vodka

Fine sea salt

Freshly ground black or white pepper

OYSTERS ON THE HALF SHELL

12 oysters, scrubbed

LEMONY FRISÉE

1 small head of frisée, separated into individual leaves

1 lemon

Fine sea salt

Freshly ground black pepper

STORE-BOUGHT COMPONENTS

3 slices of sourdough or white bread

Good-quality salted butter

1 lemon

Make the mignonette: Stir together the shallot, vinegar, vodka, a pinch of salt, and several grinds of pepper. Cover and chill for at least 20 minutes in the refrigerator before serving.

Prepare the oysters: Fold a paper towel and place it in the middle of a serving plate with a lip or in a shallow serving bowl (this will prevent the ice from sliding around). Fill a food processor about halfway with ice cubes and pulse until the ice is pebble-size. Make a bed of the crushed ice on top of the paper towel in the serving dish.

Shuck the oysters: Take one oyster at a time, find the belly side (the side that is less flat), and place the oyster belly-side down on a folded kitchen towel. Fold the towel over the oyster and hold it down with your nondominant hand. Insert the tip of an oyster knife into the hinge of the oyster (that's the V-shaped end). Twist and pry until the oyster pops open. Remove the towel, wipe the knife on it to clean the blade, then slide the oyster knife along the inside edge of the top shell to sever the muscle that holds the oyster closed. Pull off and discard the top shell. Inspect the oyster for any stray shell fragments. Slide the knife under the oyster to free it from the bottom shell. Carefully balance the oyster with its liquor in the half shell on the bed of crushed ice. The oysters should be shucked as close to serving time as possible.

Dress the frisée: Just before serving, place the frisée in a medium bowl. Add the finely grated zest from half of the lemon and a big squeeze of lemon juice, being careful to not let any seeds drop into the lettuces. Season with a pinch of salt and several grinds of pepper. Toss well.

Prepare the other components: Toast the bread and generously butter it. Cut into triangles. Cut the lemon into wedges.

Assemble: Place the plate of oysters on their bed of ice in the center of a large platter. Serve the vodka mignonette sauce in a small bowl with a little spoon. (You can nestle the bowl of sauce into the ice to keep it well chilled.) Place the buttered toast, lemony frisée, and lemon wedges alongside.

korean bbq

bulgogi-style beef + lettuce cups with so many herbs + gochujang dipping sauce + kimchi

Serves 4 to 6 • Bulgogi beef has a touch of sweetness thanks to puréed pear in the marinade. (Fun fact: The fruit also tenderizes the meat!) You want to slice the beef as thinly as possible. Freezing the whole steak for about one hour helps to firm it up before cutting, and the meat needs to marinate for at least 30 minutes, so make sure to plan ahead.

BULGOGI-STYLE BEEF

1¼ pounds (565 g) boneless beef sirloin or tenderloin

1 small yellow onion

½ Asian pear or large regular pear, peeled, cored, and coarsely chopped

3 garlic cloves

1-inch (2.5 cm) piece of fresh ginger, peeled and coarsely chopped

6 tablespoons (90 ml) soy sauce or tamari

3 tablespoons sesame oil

2 tablespoons light or dark brown sugar

¼ teaspoon freshly ground black pepper

1 tablespoon vegetable oil

1 teaspoon white sesame seeds

GOCHUJANG DIPPING SAUCE

Makes about ⅓ cup (80 ml)

¼ cup (60 ml) gochujang

1 tablespoon rice vinegar

1 tablespoon sesame oil

(ingredients continue on next page)

STORE-BOUGHT
COMPONENTS

8 ounces (225 g)
kimchi

1 head of butter
lettuce

2 handfuls of fresh
cilantro leaves and
tender stems, thinly
sliced

1 handful of fresh
perilla leaves or mint
leaves, thinly sliced

Start the bulgogi: Place the meat in a large ziptop plastic bag and chill in the freezer for 1 hour. This will make it easier to slice super thin.

Once the beef is semifrozen and firm, place it on a clean cutting board. Cut the beef across the grain as thinly as possible, ideally less than 1/8 inch (3 mm) thick. Return the meat to the ziptop bag and set aside while you make the marinade.

Thinly slice half of the onion and add it to the bag with the sliced beef. Coarsely chop the other half of the onion and place it in the bowl of a food processor along with the pear, garlic, and ginger. Blend until puréed. Pour this marinade into the bag. Add the soy sauce, sesame oil, brown sugar, and pepper. Gently squeeze the bag to mix well. Refrigerate for at least 30 minutes and up to 24 hours.

Make the dipping sauce: In a small serving bowl, stir together the gochujang, vinegar, and sesame oil until fully combined.

Prepare the other components: Place the kimchi in a small dish. Separate the head of butter lettuce into individual leaves and arrange them on a serving platter.

Finish the bulgogi: When you're ready to cook the beef, heat the vegetable oil in a cast-iron skillet over high heat for 2 minutes. Add the meat, onions, and all of the marinade liquid from the bag to the pan. Cook, stirring occasionally, until the liquid evaporates and the meat browns around the edges, 15 to 25 minutes. Sprinkle with the sesame seeds.

Assemble: Serve the hot bulgogi in the lettuce cups and scatter the cilantro and perilla over the meat. Place the dish of kimchi and the bowl of gochujang dipping sauce on the platter as well.

chicken dinner, see page 112

chicken dinner

popcorn chicken   +   cornbread bites   +   hot honey   +   homemade ranch

+   carrots and celery   +   cabbage ribbons

Serves 8 to 10   Frying bite-size pieces of popcorn chicken is much easier than frying whole chicken legs because you don't need nearly as much hot oil. Plus, who doesn't love the snackable size? The accompanying cornbread bakes directly in the skillet that you use to melt and brown the butter for the batter, making it a no-fuss dish. Store-bought ranch is totally fine if you don't want to make your own.

POPCORN CHICKEN

4 boneless, skinless chicken breasts (about 2 pounds/900 g total)

1 quart (960 ml) buttermilk

8 teaspoons fine sea salt

Freshly ground black pepper

1 quart (960 ml) vegetable oil, for frying

4 cups (500 g) all-purpose flour

2 tablespoons plus 2 teaspoons smoked paprika (sweet or hot)

4 teaspoons baking powder

CORNBREAD

Makes one (12-inch/30 cm) skillet

½ cup (1 stick/115 g) unsalted butter

2 cups (250 g) all-purpose flour

2 cups (300 g) medium-grind cornmeal

¼ cup (50 g) sugar

1 tablespoon baking powder

¼ teaspoon baking soda

2 teaspoons fine sea salt

2 large eggs

2½ cups (600 ml) buttermilk

3 tablespoons honey

HOMEMADE RANCH

1 garlic clove

Fine sea salt

1 cup (285 g) Greek yogurt

¼ cup (5 g) fresh flat-leaf parsley leaves, finely chopped

3 tablespoons fresh dill, finely chopped

2 tablespoons chopped chives

1 tablespoon lemon juice

¼ teaspoon smoked paprika (sweet or hot)

Freshly ground black pepper

STORE-BOUGHT COMPONENTS

½ small head of green cabbage

½ lemon

Chile-infused hot honey or regular honey

2 large carrots (about 300 g), cut lengthwise into quarters and then crosswise into 3-inch (7.5 cm) sticks

4 large celery stalks, cut lengthwise and then crosswise into 3-inch (7.5 cm) sticks

Start the popcorn chicken: Cut the chicken into bite-size pieces, about 1-inch (2.5 cm) cubes, and place them in a large bowl. Add the buttermilk, 4 teaspoons of the salt, and several grinds of pepper. Cover and refrigerate for at least 1 hour and up to 24 hours.

Bake the cornbread: Heat the oven to 400°F (200°C).

In a 12-inch (30 cm) oven-safe skillet, cook the butter over medium heat until it turns a deep grizzly-bear brown and smells nutty, 4 to 5 minutes. Remove the skillet from the heat and set aside.

In a very large bowl, stir together the flour, cornmeal, sugar, baking powder, baking soda, and salt. In another large bowl, whisk the eggs until frothy, then whisk the buttermilk and honey into the eggs. Pour the buttermilk mixture into the cornmeal mixture and stir gently until only a few lumps remain. Mix in the browned butter from the skillet, then pour the batter into the (already buttered!) skillet. Bake until the cornbread is evenly browned and set, 20 to 30 minutes. Let cool in the skillet.

Make the ranch: Using a mortar and pestle or the side of a large knife, crush the garlic and a pinch of salt into a paste. Transfer to a bowl and stir in the yogurt, parsley, dill, chives, lemon juice, paprika, several grinds of pepper, and ½ teaspoon of salt. Mix well. Taste and add more salt if needed. Ranch can be made ahead and stored in an airtight container in the refrigerator for up to 3 days.

Finish the popcorn chicken: When you're ready to fry the chicken, line a baking sheet with paper towels or place a wire rack over a baking sheet and set aside.

In a heavy-bottomed pot, pour the vegetable oil (or at least enough to fill the pot with 3 inches/7.5 cm of oil) and heat to 350°F (180°C). Use a probe-style instant-read thermometer to test the heat. If you don't have a thermometer, stick the handle of a wooden spoon into the oil; if bubbles form around the wood and float to the surface, the oil is ready. The oil usually takes about 10 minutes to heat.

While the oil heats up, combine the flour, paprika, baking powder, the remaining 4 teaspoons of salt, and several grinds of pepper in a medium bowl. Working in 2 or 3 batches, lift the chicken pieces out of the buttermilk and toss them in the seasoned flour. Make sure the flour coating really sticks to the meat and forms a thick crust. You can use your hands or tongs to toss the chicken in the seasoned flour. Either tool will end up coated as well, but it's worth it to make sure the chicken pieces have a nice, thick crust. Use a slotted spoon to carefully lower the coated chicken pieces into the hot oil, adding only as many as you can fit without crowding the pan. Fry until golden brown and cooked through, 3 to 5 minutes. To test if the chicken is done, cut a piece in half to see if it's opaque white all the way through. Use tongs to transfer the fried chicken to the prepared baking sheet to drain. Repeat this process to cook the remaining chicken.

Prepare the other components: Slice the cabbage into ½-inch (1 cm) ribbons and toss them in a bowl with a big squeeze of lemon juice and 2 pinches of salt.

Assemble: Transfer the popcorn chicken to a large serving platter. Cut the cornbread into two-bite squares and pile them next to the chicken. Serve the hot honey in a small bowl with a little spoon. Arrange the cabbage on the side with toothpicks so that when you are craving something cold and bright between bites of fried chicken, you can use a toothpick to spear a lemony cabbage ribbon. Spoon the ranch into its own small bowl and place the carrots and celery nearby for dipping.

HOW TO MAKE AHEAD

Popcorn chicken can be kept warm in a single layer on a baking sheet (no paper towels!) in a 200°F (90°C) oven for up to 1 hour. It can also be fried ahead, stored in the refrigerator for a day or two, and reheated in a single layer on a baking sheet in a 350°F (180°C) oven until warmed through and crisp on the outside, about 10 minutes.

smørrebrød-esque

smoked salmon + caper berry cream cheese spread + pickled green onions + crackers

Serves 2 to 4 • Caper berries come from the same plant as capers but have a distinct flavor that is reminiscent of mustard. The berries are about the size of large grapes, and you can find jars of them in the condiments aisle. For this Scandinavian-inspired board, they're chopped and mixed into cream cheese for a spread that pairs perfectly with the smoky flavor of the salmon and the tangy pickled green onions.

PICKLED GREEN ONIONS

¼ cup (60 ml) rice vinegar, apple cider vinegar, or white wine vinegar

¼ cup (60 ml) water

½ teaspoon sugar

¼ teaspoon fine sea salt

1 teaspoon black peppercorns

6 green onions, white and green parts cut into ¼-inch (6 mm) slices

CAPER BERRY CREAM CHEESE

Makes about ½ cup (115 g)

½ cup (4 ounces/ 115 g) cream cheese, at room temperature

7 caper berries, stemmed and finely chopped, plus a few whole berries for garnish

2 tablespoons fresh lemon juice

Fine sea salt

Freshly ground black pepper

STORE-BOUGHT COMPONENTS

3 ounces (85 g) smoked salmon

Dark brown flatbread-style crackers, with or without fruit

Pickle the green onions: In a small nonreactive pot, combine the vinegar, water, sugar, salt, and peppercorns. Bring to a boil. Remove the pot from the heat, add the green onions, and let them soak until cool. Pickled green onions can be enjoyed immediately or transferred with some of the brine to a 1-cup (240 ml) jar, covered with an airtight lid, and stored in the fridge for up to 3 weeks.

Make the caper berry cream cheese: Stir together the cream cheese, chopped caper berries, and lemon juice. Season with a pinch of salt and plenty of black pepper.

Assemble: Spoon the caper berry cream cheese into a small bowl and place it on a serving board (with a small knife for spreading). Arrange the smoked salmon, crackers, and whole caper berries to the side. Serve the pickled green onions in a little bowl with a spoon or toothpicks.

spicy herby kofta

lamb kofta   +   yogurt-mint sauce   +   herb salad   +   pita bread

Serves 2 to 4 • These lamb meatballs on skewers are boldly flavored with cumin, sumac, and harissa. The accompanying dipping sauce is both spicy and cooling—fresh green chile brings the heat and creamy yogurt balances it. You'll have some sauce left over, but it's delicious served with all kinds of grilled meat or cooked vegetables, especially the Cauliflower Pakoras (page 39).

YOGURT-MINT SAUCE

Makes about 1½ cups (375 g)

1 cup (250 g) plain whole-milk yogurt

2 cups (40 g) fresh mint leaves

1 small, fresh hot green chile, stemmed and seeded

2 tablespoons fresh lime juice

2 teaspoons light or dark brown sugar

½ teaspoon fine sea salt

Freshly ground black pepper

LAMB KOFTA

Makes 10 small meatballs

1 garlic clove

1 teaspoon cumin seeds

8 ounces (225 g) ground lamb

¼ cup (5 g) fresh cilantro leaves, finely chopped

1 tablespoon harissa

2 teaspoons sumac

1 large egg

½ teaspoon fine sea salt

Freshly ground black pepper

1 tablespoon extra-virgin olive oil

STORE-BOUGHT COMPONENTS

Stack of pita bread, warmed

¼ cup (5 g) fresh mint leaves

¼ cup (5 g) fresh cilantro leaves

½ lime

Make the yogurt-mint sauce: Spoon the yogurt into a shallow serving bowl. In a blender or food processor, combine the mint, chile, lime juice, brown sugar, salt, and several grinds of pepper. Pulse until very finely chopped. Spoon the mint mixture onto the yogurt; you can leave as is or stir the two together. Chill in the refrigerator until ready to serve.

Make the kofta: Using a mortar and pestle or the side of a large knife, crush the garlic into a paste. Mix the cumin into the garlic paste and smash the two together until the cumin is coarsely ground. Transfer the garlic-cumin paste to a medium bowl and add the lamb, cilantro, harissa, sumac, egg, salt, and lots of pepper. Mix well to combine (your hands are the best tool for this step—they will help distribute the seasoning evenly throughout the meat), then shape into 10 golf-ball-size meatballs. Pierce each meatball with a little, flat wooden skewer, then mold each into an oval shape around the skewer for the classic kofta look. (If you don't have little skewers, don't worry, the kofta will be just as delicious.)

Heat a large skillet over medium-high heat for 2 minutes. Swirl in the oil, then cook the meatballs until browned on one side, 3 to 4 minutes. Turn and cook on the other side until just cooked through, another 4 minutes or so.

Assemble: Serve the kofta on a platter or board with the bowl of yogurt-mint sauce for dipping. Stack the pita (whole or cut into wedges) alongside. Arrange the mint and cilantro leaves in a little pile. Squeeze some lime juice over the herbs and season them with a pinch of salt and several grinds of pepper.

sweet

holiday cookie swap

lemon-rosemary shortbread   +   chocolate bark   +   gluten-free coconut macaroons

Serves 6 to 8   •   This lemon-rosemary shortbread requires only five ingredients plus salt, and, like the chocolate bark, can be prepared ahead. Make both for a festive cookie swap with friends and pick up another kind of cookie (like gluten-free coconut macaroons) from a local bakery to fill out the board.

LEMON-ROSEMARY SHORTBREAD

Makes 20 cookies

2 cups (250 g) all-purpose flour, plus more for rolling

Finely grated zest of 2 lemons

2 tablespoons fresh rosemary leaves, finely chopped

1 teaspoon fine sea salt

1 cup (2 sticks/ 225 g) unsalted butter, at room temperature

⅔ cup (135 g) sugar

CHOCOLATE BARK

Makes 20 pieces

¼ cup (35 g) almonds

¼ cup (35 g) pistachios

¼ cup (30 g) hulled pumpkin seeds (aka pepitas)

10½ ounces (300 g) bittersweet chocolate, chopped into small pieces

¼ cup (40 g) dried cherries or dried cranberries

STORE-BOUGHT COMPONENTS

Gluten-free coconut macaroons, or any cookie of your choice

Make the shortbread: In a large bowl, stir together the flour, lemon zest, rosemary, and salt.

In another large bowl, vigorously mix the butter and sugar using a wooden spoon until creamy and lightened in color, about 3 minutes. (Alternatively, you can use a stand mixer fitted with the paddle attachment.) Add the flour mixture and mix until just combined. Gather the dough into a ball, wrap tightly in plastic wrap, and refrigerate for 30 minutes.

About 15 minutes before you're ready to bake the cookies, heat the oven to 300°F (150°C) and line a baking sheet with parchment paper.

On a lightly floured surface, roll out the dough to ½-inch (1 cm) thickness. Cut into 20 rectangles, about 2 inches (5 cm) wide (or any shape you like as long as they are approximately the same size), and place them on the prepared baking sheet, leaving space between each one. Bake until lightly golden brown, 30 to 35 minutes, rotating the baking sheet halfway through. Transfer the shortbread to a wire rack and let cool completely. You can store the cookies in an airtight container for up to 1 week.

Make the chocolate bark: Heat the oven to 350°F (180°C) and line a rimmed baking sheet with parchment paper.

Place the almonds, pistachios, and pumpkin seeds on the baking sheet. Toast in the oven until fragrant, about 10 minutes. Transfer the nuts and seeds to a cutting board and coarsely chop them. Set aside to cool. Keep the lined baking sheet for the chocolate bark.

Meanwhile, in a medium saucepan, bring about 1 inch (2.5 cm) of water to a simmer. Set a heatproof bowl over the pan (make sure the bottom of the bowl does not touch the water). Place the chocolate in the bowl and gently heat, stirring occasionally, until fully melted. Remove the bowl from the heat, taking care not to splash any water into the chocolate.

Pour the melted chocolate onto the lined baking sheet and use a rubber spatula to spread it out to an approximately 8 by 10-inch (20 by 25 cm) rectangle. Scatter the nuts and seeds over the chocolate, then scatter the dried cherries on top. Use your fingertips to gently press the cherries into the chocolate. Let the chocolate cool at room temperature until it sets, about 2 hours, or chill it in the refrigerator until firm. (The fridge is much speedier, but sometimes fluctuations in humidity can cause the chocolate to discolor.) Use a large knife to cut the bark into about 20 irregular-shaped pieces. Chocolate bark can be stored in an airtight container at room temperature for up to 2 weeks.

Assemble: Arrange the lemon-rosemary shortbread, chocolate bark pieces, and coconut macaroons on a board or platter.

chocolate deluxe, see page 130

chocolate deluxe

tahini swirl brownies + chocolate-dipped strawberries + chocolate-hazelnut spread + pretzels +

dark chocolate truffles + chocolate–peanut butter cups + mixed nuts + figs + plums

Serves 8 to 10 • To all the chocolate lovers out there, this board is for you. Chocolate is an ingredient whose quality varies greatly, so make sure to buy the highest quality you can afford. The greater the cocoa percentage, the more intensely chocolaty and less sweet the flavor will be. Feel free to use your favorite kind (dark, bittersweet, milk, or white) for the chocolate-dipped strawberries.

TAHINI SWIRL BROWNIES

Makes 25 bite-size squares

12 tablespoons (1½ sticks/170 g) unsalted butter

6 ounces (170 g) unsweetened chocolate, chopped into small pieces

2 cups (400 g) granulated sugar

2 teaspoons pure vanilla extract

3 large eggs

1 cup (125 g) all-purpose flour

½ teaspoon flaky sea salt

2 ounces (55 g) white chocolate, chopped into small pieces

¼ cup (60 g) tahini

CHOCOLATE-HAZELNUT SPREAD

Makes 2 cups (480 ml)

2 cups (280 g) hazelnuts

¼ cup (60 ml) plus 2 tablespoons hazelnut oil or neutral-flavored vegetable oil

3 tablespoons unsweetened cocoa powder

3 tablespoons confectioners' sugar

1½ teaspoons pure vanilla extract

½ teaspoon fine sea salt

CHOCOLATE-DIPPED STRAWBERRIES

Makes about 12

1 pint (290 g) strawberries

5 ounces (140 g) bittersweet chocolate, chopped

STORE-BOUGHT COMPONENTS

Dark chocolate truffles

Mini milk chocolate–peanut butter cups

Bite-size salted pretzels

1½ cups (175 g) roasted salted mixed nuts

4 or 5 figs, cut into halves or quarters

2 or 3 plums, sliced into wedges

Bake the brownies: Heat the oven to 350°F (180°C). Line an 8-inch (20 cm) square baking dish with parchment paper, allowing the paper to overhang the sides a bit so that you can easily lift out the brownies.

Bring about 1 inch (2.5 cm) of water to a simmer in a small saucepan. Set a large heatproof bowl over the pot (make sure the bottom of the bowl doesn't touch the water). Place the butter and unsweetened chocolate in the bowl and heat gently, stirring occasionally, until melted and well combined. Remove the bowl from the heat, taking care not to splash any water into the chocolate. Leave the pot with the water on the stovetop.

Add the sugar, vanilla, and eggs to the melted butter and chocolate mixture and whisk vigorously for several minutes until very smooth. Stir in the flour and flaky salt. Using a rubber spatula, scrape the batter into the prepared pan and spread it evenly.

Bring the water in the saucepan to a simmer once again. Set a clean bowl over the pot (again make sure the bottom of the bowl doesn't touch the water). Place the white chocolate in the bowl and heat gently, stirring occasionally, until just barely melted. Be careful not to overheat the white chocolate or it might thicken. Remove the bowl from the heat.

Dollop small spoonfuls of the melted white chocolate on the surface of the brownie batter in about 10 different places. Use a clean spoon to dollop the tahini in 10 different places. Using a skewer or toothpick, swirl them to create a marble pattern.

Bake until puffed and just barely set, 50 to 55 minutes, depending on how done you like your brownies. They will look slightly domed in the pan (and may have cracked or bubbled across the marble surface) and will feel set, not liquidy, when tapped lightly with your finger. A toothpick inserted into the center won't come out clean; the brownies will still be gooey immediately after baking but will set a little further as they cool to room temperature. Let them cool in the pan, then remove them using the parchment paper and cut into bite-size squares.

Store leftover brownies, tightly wrapped or in an airtight container, at room temperature for up to 3 days.

Make the chocolate-hazelnut spread: Heat the oven to 350°F (180°C).

Place the hazelnuts on a rimmed baking sheet. Toast in the oven until they're fragrant and lightly browned, 12 to 15 minutes. Wrap the nuts in a clean kitchen towel and rub them to remove as much of their papery skins as possible.

While the hazelnuts are still warm, use a food processor or high-speed blender to grind them and ¼ cup (60 ml) of the hazelnut oil to a smooth hazelnut butter, stopping the machine and scraping down the sides every minute or so, 4 to 10 minutes total, depending on your machine. Add the cocoa powder, sugar, vanilla, fine salt, and the remaining 2 tablespoons hazelnut oil. Blend until fully incorporated. The mixture will be a little looser and more rustic than Nutella, but that's to be expected because it doesn't have any of the added emulsifiers. Transfer the spread to a 1-pint (480 ml) jar or two 1-cup (240 ml) jars. Enjoy right away or store, covered, at room temperature for up to 2 weeks.

Make the chocolate-dipped strawberries: Line a baking sheet with parchment paper and set aside. Rinse the strawberries and dry them very well. It is important there are no droplets of water clinging to the berries; otherwise, the chocolate will slide right off.

In a small saucepan, bring about 1 inch (2.5 cm) of water to a simmer. Set a heatproof bowl over the pot (make sure the bottom of the bowl does not touch the water). Place the bittersweet chocolate in the bowl and heat gently, stirring occasionally, until melted. Remove the bowl from the heat, taking care not to splash any water into the chocolate. Hold a strawberry by the stem and dip it into the melted chocolate, rotating the berry to coat all sides evenly. Set the chocolate-dipped strawberry on the prepared baking sheet. Repeat with the other berries. Place the baking sheet in the refrigerator to chill until the chocolate sets, about 15 minutes.

Assemble: Arrange the brownie bites and chocolate-dipped strawberries on a large board along with the dark chocolate truffles and chocolate–peanut butter cups. Serve the chocolate-hazelnut spread in a bowl, with pretzels alongside for dipping. Place the mixed nuts in another bowl and nestle the figs and plums in any empty spaces on the board.

autumn harvest

sugared grapes + green apples + salted caramel sauce + candied walnut crunch

Serves 4 to 6 • This sweet board celebrates the fruits of autumn and pairs them with homemade salted caramel sauce and store-bought candied walnuts. Making your own caramel sauce is quick and simple. Serve it warm with green apple slices for dipping (and save any extra for pouring over ice cream).

SUGARED GRAPES

½ cup (120 ml) water

1 cup (200 g) sugar

1 pound (455 g) red or green seedless grapes, stemmed

SALTED CARAMEL SAUCE

Makes about 1 cup (240 ml)

1 cup (200 g) sugar

6 tablespoons (¾ stick/85 g) unsalted butter, at room temperature

½ cup (120 ml) heavy cream

¾ teaspoon fine sea salt

STORE-BOUGHT COMPONENTS

2 or 3 green apples

½ cup (60 g) candied walnuts

Sugar the grapes: Set a wire rack inside a rimmed baking sheet. In a small saucepan, combine the water and ½ cup (100 g) of the sugar. Bring to a simmer, stirring frequently, until the sugar dissolves completely. Remove the pan from the heat, add the grapes, and stir until they are evenly coated in syrup. Using a slotted spoon, transfer the grapes to the prepared rack and spread them apart from one another so they aren't touching. Let sit at room temperature, until the syrup forms a sticky coating on the grapes, about 1 hour.

Spread the remaining ½ cup (100 g) sugar on a small plate. Working with a few grapes at a time, roll them in the sugar and return them to the rack. Once you've done this with all the grapes, set aside until ready to serve.

Make the caramel: Heat the sugar in a medium saucepan over medium heat, stirring often with a heatproof rubber spatula. The sugar will first crystallize into chunks, but keep stirring and eventually the sugar will transform into a liquidy syrup. It will be clear at first, then it'll turn golden and become progressively darker in color. As soon as the syrup is an amber color, carefully add the butter (the mixture will bubble!). Continue cooking and stirring until the butter is completely melted. While stirring, slowly pour in the cream (be careful, it will bubble again). Cook for 1 minute, then remove the pan from the heat and stir in the salt. Transfer the salted caramel sauce to a jar and let cool slightly. Caramel can be made ahead and stored, covered, in the refrigerator for up to 2 weeks. Reheat gently before serving.

Prepare the other components: Just before serving, core and slice the apples. Finely chop the candied walnuts and place them in a small bowl for sprinkling or dipping.

Assemble: Serve the caramel sauce in its jar or in a small bowl on a platter and arrange the sliced apples to the side along with the candied walnut crunch and the sugared grapes.

s'mores
without a campfire

---

graham crackers   +   toasted marshmallows   +   warm chocolate sauce

---

Serves 4 to 6 • Your oven broiler or gas stovetop can stand in for a smoky campfire here, browning the marshmallows until they're perfectly toasted. To complete the s'mores board setup, a warm chocolate sauce is just the right texture for dipping. Homemade Nutella, aka Chocolate-Hazelnut Spread (page 130), wouldn't be bad either.

CHOCOLATE SAUCE

Makes about 1 cup (240 ml)

½ cup (120 ml) water

⅓ cup (30 g) unsweetened cocoa powder

½ cup (100 g) sugar

Pinch of fine sea salt

2 ounces (55 g) bittersweet chocolate, finely chopped

TOASTED MARSHMALLOWS

12 large marshmallows

STORE-BOUGHT COMPONENTS

Graham crackers

Make the chocolate sauce: In a small or medium saucepan, whisk together the water, cocoa powder, sugar, and salt over medium heat. Once the mixture boils, remove the pan from the heat and add the chocolate. Stir until the chocolate dissolves. The chocolate sauce will thicken as it cools. Serve it when it's warm and dippable but not so hot it's runny. Any extra will keep in a jar in the fridge for up to 1 week, ready to be gently rewarmed and spooned over your next ice cream sundae.

Toast the marshmallows: Just before you're ready to serve the board, heat the oven broiler to high. Line a baking sheet with aluminum foil. Lay the marshmallows on the sheet in a single layer. Place under the broiler until golden brown and toasted on one side, about 15 seconds. Carefully flip the marshmallows and broil on another side until golden brown and toasted, 15 seconds. Continue flipping and broiling until the marshmallows are golden brown on a few sides. (Alternatively, you can stick wooden skewers in the marshmallows and cook them over a gas stovetop until toasted on a few sides.)

Assemble: Arrange the toasted marshmallows on a serving board. Stack the graham crackers next to them and serve the warm chocolate sauce in a small bowl with a little spoon.

high tea

hibiscus-glazed scones + barely whipped cream + berry jam + fresh fruit

Serves 4 to 8 • These lemony scones are glazed with vivid fuchsia icing. The beautiful natural color comes from dried hibiscus flowers, which you can find in Mexican markets. (Alternatively, you can use a hibiscus tea bag.) Choose any fresh fruit you love for this board. A combination of a few different fruits will look the most visually striking.

SCONES

Makes 8

¼ cup (50 g) granulated sugar

1 lemon

2 cups (250 g) all-purpose flour

¼ cup (30 g) whole-wheat flour

1½ teaspoons baking powder

½ teaspoon fine sea salt

¼ teaspoon baking soda

½ cup (1 stick/115 g) unsalted butter, very cold and cut into 8 pieces

¾ cup (180 ml) very cold heavy cream, plus more as needed

1 teaspoon pure vanilla extract

HIBISCUS GLAZE

1 tablespoon dried hibiscus flowers (aka flor de jamaica) or 1 hibiscus tea bag

1 cup (125 g) confectioners' sugar, sifted

Pinch of fine sea salt

BARELY WHIPPED CREAM

1 cup (240 ml) heavy cream

2 teaspoons confectioners' sugar

1 teaspoon pure vanilla extract

STORE-BOUGHT COMPONENTS

Good-quality berry jam

Fresh fruit (such as cherries, nectarines, and apricots)

Bake the scones: Heat the oven to 400°F (200°C). Line a baking sheet with parchment paper.

In a small bowl, combine the granulated sugar and the finely grated zest of the lemon. (Save the zested lemon for the glaze.) Using your fingers, rub the zest into the sugar until fragrant, about 1 minute.

In a large bowl, stir together the all-purpose flour, whole-wheat flour, baking powder, salt, and baking soda. Add the lemony sugar to the bowl and stir to combine. Add the butter and, using your fingertips, rub the butter into the mixture until there are no butter pieces larger than a pea. Pour in the cream and vanilla. Stir with a wooden spoon to form a crumbly dough. If the dough is too floury and won't come together, add more cream, 1 tablespoon at a time, until it just barely holds together. Turn it out onto an unfloured surface and knead quickly to bring the dough completely together. Fold it in half onto itself, as if you were closing a book, then pat and shape the dough into a circle that is 1 inch (2.5 cm) thick. Using a large knife, cut the dough into 8 triangles and transfer them to the prepared baking sheet.

Bake the scones until lightly browned around the bottom edges, 15 to 20 minutes. Transfer them to a wire rack to cool.

Make the glaze: Squeeze the juice from the reserved zested lemon into a small saucepan. Add the hibiscus flowers (or the tea bag, if using) and warm gently over medium heat until the flowers impart their fuchsia color to the lemon juice. Once the lemon juice is hot, you can remove the pan from the heat and let the hibiscus steep until the color is pronounced; about 5 minutes of steeping should do the trick. Strain into a small bowl and discard the flowers (or tea bag).

In another small bowl, combine the confectioners' sugar and salt. Stir 1 tablespoon of the hibiscus-infused lemon juice into the sugar. Gradually add more juice, 1 teaspoon at a time, until the glaze is thick but pourable. Drizzle the glaze over the cooled scones or serve it in a bowl alongside.

Whip the cream: In a medium bowl, whisk the cream, confectioners' sugar, and vanilla by hand or using electric beaters until the cream thickens and holds very soft, floppy peaks.

Assemble: Transfer the barely whipped cream to a serving bowl and place it on a platter next to the scones. Spoon the berry jam into a small serving bowl and set it alongside with any desired serving utensils. Arrange the fresh fruit around the other components.

honey and halva

Serves 6 to 8 • Sweet dates, fresh figs, and bakery-bought baklava go together happily on this platter. Choose large Medjool dates for stuffing with the halva filling; smaller date varieties like Deglet Noor are a little trickier to fill, although no less delicious if that's all you can find.

HALVA-STUFFED DATES

3 ounces (85 g) vanilla halva or plain halva

2 tablespoons tahini

1 tablespoon honey

1 to 2 tablespoons ice water

12 large Medjool dates

1 tablespoon pistachios, very finely chopped

Flaky sea salt

STORE-BOUGHT COMPONENTS

8 ounces (225 g) baklava

3 ounces (85 g) honeycomb

Fresh figs, halved or quartered, or sliced oranges (not pictured)

Make the halva-stuffed dates: Use a food processor to blend the halva, tahini, and honey until combined. Add 1 tablespoon of the ice water and blend to incorporate. Scrape down the sides and across the bottom of the food processor bowl—the halva likes to hide out in the crevices. Blend again until fully incorporated. If the mixture isn't moving around the bowl of the food processor, add a little ice water, but no more than an additional 1 tablespoon. Cut each date lengthwise, remove and discard the pit, and spoon in enough halva filling to completely fill the date. Scatter the chopped pistachios across the stuffed dates and sprinkle with flaky salt.

Assemble: Serve the halva-stuffed dates on a board or platter along with the baklava, honeycomb (with a small serving knife), and figs.

SOURCES

There aren't any recipes in this book that require specific brands of ingredients. But if you're looking for a little direction in terms of finding store-bought components, here are some favorite producers to keep your eye out for.

ANCHOVIES AND OTHER TINNED FISH

Ortiz
conservasortiz.com

Wild Planet
wildplanetfoods.com

CHEESE AND OTHER DAIRY PRODUCTS

Bellwether Farms
bellwetherfarms.com

Cowgirl Creamery Cheese Shop
cowgirlcreamery.com

Laura Chenel's Chèvre, Inc.
laurachenel.com

Meredith Dairy (for marinated cheese)
meredithdairy.com

Murray's
murrayscheese.com

Point Reyes Farmstead Cheese Co.
pointreyescheese.com

CHIPS AND CRACKERS

Casa Sanchez
casasanchezsf.com

Judy's Sesame Breadsticks
lovesticks.com

La Panzanella
lapanzanella.com

Potter's Crackers
potterscrackers.com

Rustic Bakery
rusticbakery.com

Vegetable Chips
Rhythm Superfoods Carrot Sticks
rhythmsuperfoods.com

Treasure 8's Beet Chips
treasure8.com

**CHOCOLATE AND
COCOA POWDER**
Guittard Chocolate Company
guittard.com

Valrhona
valrhona-chocolate.com

DATES
Rancho Meladuco
ranchomeladuco.com

HALVA
Halvah Heaven
halvah-heaven.myshopify.com

Hebel & Co.
hebelco.com

HARISSA
New York Shuk
nyshuk.com

GOCHUJANG
Mother-in-Law's
milkimchi.com

Rhei-Maid
rheimaid.com

HONEY AND HONEYCOMB
Bees Knees
bushwickkitchen.com

Bee Local
beelocal.com

Bee Raw
beeraw.com

Jacobsen Salt Co.
jacobsensalt.com

Savannah Bee Company
savannahbee.com

Wedderspoon
wedderspoon.com

Zach & Zoë Sweet Bee Farm
zachandzoe.co

**JAMS, CHUTNEY,
AND OTHER PRESERVES**
Akka's Handcrafted Foods
(for mango chutney)
myakkas.com

Crofter's Organic
croftersorganic.com

Happy Girl Kitchen Co.
happygirlkitchen.com

INNA
innajam.com

June Taylor
junetaylorjams.com

JARRED PEPPERS

Jeff's Garden
jeffsgardenfoods.com

MARCONA ALMONDS

Matiz
matizespana.com

OIL

California Olive Ranch
californiaoliveranch.com

Enzo Olive Oil
enzooliveoil.com

Exau
exauoliveoil.com

Pineapple Collaborative
pineapplecollaborative.com

Séka Hills
sekahills.com

La Tourangelle
(for hazelnut oil)
latourangelle.com

OYSTERS

Hog Island Oyster Co.
hogislandoysters.com

**PROSCIUTTO, SALUMI, AND
OTHER CURED MEATS**

Fra'Mani Handcrafted Foods
framani.com

La Quercia
laquerciashop.com

Olympia Provisions
olympiaprovisions.com

SALT AND SPICES

Burlap & Barrel
burlapandbarrel.com

Diaspora Co.
diasporaco.com

Jacobsen Salt Co.
jacobsensalt.com

Kalustyan's
kalustyans.com

Maldon Spice Company
maldonsalt.co.uk

Oaktown Spice Shop
oaktownspiceshop.com

Penzeys Spices
penzeys.com

Zingerman's
zingermans.com

TAHINI

Soom
soomfoods.com

WALNUTS

Old Dog Ranch
olddogranch.com

ACKNOWLEDGMENTS

I always read the acknowledgments of a book before I even glance at any other page. It's a habit I picked up from the days when I was dreaming of becoming a published author and I was eager and curious to learn more about the people behind books. While there's usually only one name on the cover, there are many others who help bring a book to life. Without their vital contributions, books wouldn't be as beautifully designed, edited, tested, typeset, or produced. I hope I can adequately convey my gratitude to the team of people who played a role in the creation of this cookbook.

Thank you to everyone at Artisan Books, especially publisher Lia Ronnen, whose knowledge and intuition is unparalleled. Thank you to editors Bella Lemos and Judy Pray; art director Suet Chong; production editor Carson Lombardi; copyeditor Mark McCauslin (how did I get so lucky to have you expertly copyedit my book?); the production team of Nancy Murray and Erica Huang; and publicist Theresa Collier.

Kitty Cowles, my dear friend and agent, your insight and brilliance made this book—and every book we've worked on together—better by leaps and bounds. I am still in awe that my name appears on the list of authors you represent.

Erin Scott, thank you for the gorgeous photographs and for your skill in prop styling. Neither of us could have imagined that we would be doing the photo shoot for this cookbook during a pandemic, and I will forever appreciate your flexibility, care, and drive to make it happen safely. Thanks also to the entire Scott family, particularly Lilah, for lending a hand and for letting me spend so much time in your garden and backyard. Thank you to kitchen assistant Bruce Cole for being on our quaran-team.

The recipes in this book were tested multiple times by a wonderful group affectionately known as the Testing Team. Thank you to Davita Urdang-Spencer, Gyu Park, Hannah Robie, Katie Kelley, Laura Bradley, Corinne Sengwe, Annie Zisk, Erika Lee, Jane Hausauer, Maïalène Wilkins, Celeste Saharig, Christina Billing, Courtney Cikach, Elise Carlton, Tim and Toni Carlton, Jessica Naecker, Emily Forscher, Taylor Schwartz, Amanda Sarley-Weng, Judith Mandel, Alissa Rimmon, Claire Bray, Ali Stieglitz, Edith Williams, Yoon Hur, Hollie Loson, Jessa Strayer, Alice Mount, Alyson Parkes, Lena Gebhard, Sonja Hernandez, Juliana Stone and Jared Stone, Rachel Hochstetler, Rena Kolhede, Alana Buckley, Erica Wrightson, Christine Binder, Dawn Nita, Natasha Bartolome and Ryan Hutson, Pinky Farnum, Tori Ambruso, Alexa Prendergast, Pam Pauley, Jocelyn Bradley, Dana Washington, Carly Haase-Duester, Allie Silvas, Maggie Bromberg, Natasha Nicolai, Paula Wade, Sofia Martin, Elizabeth Rothschild, Lisa Goldstein, Sophie Tivona, Jessica Plummer, Emery Sorvino, Wendy Lee and Nick Snead, Kathryn Phelan, Sarah Franklin, Paige Hermreck, Lauren Karas, Carly Dela Cruz, Victoria Stanell, Brittney Boehm, Hannah Davitian, Jess L'Esperance, Lisa Wahl, Sara Lopez-Isaacs, Jane Feinberg, Tom Purtill, Sarah Fisher, Jaimi Boehm, Carly Hackbarth, Elizabeth Blanke, Clare Langan, Madeline Mihran, Rachial Parrish, Suzi Freitas, Taylor Lewis,

Emily Burns, Coral Lee, Alex Lentz, Colleen Wahl, Stephanie Bohar, Emily Rusca, Julie Beigel-Coryell, Jen Nurse, Ashley Lasher, Sarah Cotey, Sydney Clark, Libby Bradley, and Kate Long.

Thank you to the hardworking farmers and producers who grow, pickle, ferment, cure, bottle, bake, or otherwise make the ingredients upon which these recipes rely. You are an endless source of inspiration. Thanks also to the booksellers who've championed *The Newlywed Table* and other books of mine. It has been such a pleasure to get to know you.

I'm grateful for the opportunities to collaborate with and learn from my heroes in the kitchen, most especially Suzanne Goin, Elisabeth Prueitt, Chad Robertson, Christina Tosi, Alice Waters, Yotam Ottolenghi, Fuchsia Dunlop, Nigel Slater, Nadiya Hussain, Yasmin Khan, Fabrizia Lanza, Deborah Madison, and Roxana Jullapat. You've taught me a great deal, and I often picture you all standing in my own little kitchen, cheering me on and offering advice.

To my family and friends, thank you so much for your love and support. I hope you know that I cherish you.

Graham Willis Bradley, you are the love of my life. Without you by my side, I would never have been able to write this cookbook. Thank you for encouraging me, believing in me, and always valuing my work. Cooking with you is my favorite thing to do. If we have one hundred more years together, it won't be enough.

INDEX

MARIA ZIZKA is a cookbook writer and recipe developer who was named by Forbes as one of the most influential people under thirty in the world of food and drink. She has coauthored numerous award-winning cookbooks, including *Tartine All Day*, *Everything I Want to Eat*, and *This Is Camino*. Her first solo cookbook, *The Newlywed Table*, was published in 2019. Zizka lives and cooks in the San Francisco Bay Area. Find her on Instagram at @mariazizka.